Intelligent
Rebel
Amongst
the
Entitled

Dr. Javad Ghoreishi

CONTENTS

Preface

While this book describes real-life events, often of a traumatic and/or abusive nature, the names of many real-life figures within these pages (and their identifying information), particularly lawyers and judges, has been changed, based on their distinguishing characteristics, and so as to avoid violating any laws. However, the information contained here is of public record, and actual names and law firms can be accessed through the Norfolk County Court System's website.

Introduction

I n the year 2020, the racist underbelly of the United States legal system has made itself boldly apparent to the world at large. These systemic issues stretch far and wide. From the police brutality now seen every day on the news, to widespread mass incarceration, an ordinary person doesn't have to look far to see horrific examples of prejudice at work, as the nation's most oppressed groups are subjugated to hostility, bias, and racism in the courts.

While the world has now been forcibly made aware of the biases at work in the criminal justice system, though, these same prejudices are just as darkly apparent in other parts of the legal system, as well – including divorce trials. Few know this more than Dr. Javad Ghoreishi, a distinguished dentist living in Brookline, Massachusetts. After immigrating to the United States in 1986 following political turmoil in his home country of Iran, Dr. Javad spent decades forming a strong dental practice, a list of notable and sometimes celebrity clients, a number of pharmaceutical patents to his name, and a reputation that should have spoken for itself when, in the twenty-first century, his divorce proceedings first began. No matter how the divorce case went, Dr. Javad has proven himself to be a contributing member of society, and he deserved the utmost respect in all legal matters.

That, unfortunately, is not what happened.

Why? Because as an immigrant, and a disabled person, Dr. Javad was instead faced with racism, ableism, and bias at every turn. He was second-guessed, swept aside, and taken advantage of by lawyers such as Ms. Trash and Mr. Garbage, from Boston, a duo whom he now refers to as "vermin swindlers," while other lawyers treated him, due to his disability, as if he was less than human. Throughout the process, he argues that he was treated abysmally, and every step of the path has been arduous, with seemingly the entire system being unified against him. "I am not a dumb person," the dentist says, looking back on the matter. "I am intelligent enough to read, and to learn."

Throughout Dr. Javad's long, tangled, and tragic battles with the courts, he has had to represent himself, learn the ropes of the legal profession, and continually be dismissed or mistreated due to his background and disability. "There is only a façade of justice left at the Norfolk Probate and Family Court," he says. "For all these years, going to said court, all the guards always told me not to give up what I was doing – that I was doing the right thing. So I kept going." Today, he continues fighting, both for himself, and to try to make public the discrimination he has faced, in the hope of forging a better system. Looking on the matter today, Dr. Javad is firm and unwavering in his dedication to publicizing the events that have happened to him. He wants to make it clear, for the world, what he has been through, and he wants those whom he says have wronged him to be seen for what they are, as well. He sees the discrimination he has faced, believes that it does not align with the stated values of the United States that first brought him to this nation decades ago, and he wants to see changes happen.

As Ghoreishi puts it himself: "They let me in as an immigrant, as long as I can work as a slave. But when it comes down to it, I have no rights. I am an intelligent and educated person. I work very hard at what I do. Yet, I have been treated like a slave, both because of racism and because my disability, for I am wheelchair-bound … I want everyone to know. I want things to change."

This is his story.

1

EVERYTHING BEGINS SOMEWHERE

When one meets Dr. Javad Ghoreishi, there are a few qualities that immediately make themselves apparent. First, he is a survivor. He has clearly experienced much over the years, both good and bad, and he carries those scars with him, everywhere he goes, and into every situation. In his lifetime, he has faced a great deal of hardship, ranging from the struggles of immigrating to a new country, to the painful medical realities of multiple sclerosis, and finally, the racism he faced in the United States justice system. Dr. Javad also embodies perseverance, having long ago realized that in a system so weighted against him, he had to be his own advocate, his own source of strength, and sometimes even his own lawyer. Perhaps the quality that he most embodies, however, is not hardship, but wisdom and courage. He is a man gifted with immense intelligence, a prized dentist, and he possesses the knowledge base and humbleness to study any subject he wants to learn more about, and to challenge authority, even when he is facing seemingly insurmountable odds.

Dr. Javad is also, of course, an immigrant. As he explains, "I am originally from Iran. I was born in Iran, I studied in Iran, and I became a dentist in Iran, first … Very few students made it into the university I studied at. They had to be the cream of the crop, and I was and still am proud to be one of them."

Speaking of his beginnings in Iran, Dr. Javad describes himself as a political rebel. "I was an activist," he says. While the story of his immigration is, in his words, "a whole other book," which he does intend to write about someday, a proper understanding of his struggles in the U.S. is best framed by a basic understanding of the conditions in Iran, during the twentieth century, which first led him to escape to the United States in the first place, in search of a better life and future.

While the event now known as the Iranian Revolution occurred in 1979, its roots – as with all such events – stretched a great deal further back, due to foreign intervention, who installed and supported the monarchy of Reza Shah Pahlavi, and the resulting Pahlavi dynasty. This entire situation exploded in the late seventies, as Pahlavi rule was overthrown, and he was replaced with the Grand Ayatollah Rolhollah Khomeimi. The details regarding the revolution are, indeed, complex and multifaceted – as Dr. Javad says, definitely enough to fill an entire book—but one key aspect is that while there was a number of groups who supported overthrowing the monarchy, these same groups did not support the religiously extreme, theocratic rule that took over afterward. This culminated in attacks on protesters, the shutting down of democratic norms, and the closing of universities and the newspapers of their opponents.

Speaking of his own experiences, Dr. Javad is quite blunt about his feelings on the matter: "They [the regime] brutally massacred all of their political and cultural opponents, which therefore forced a large number of highly educated intellectuals, to leave their home country, with their families, including political activists, political opponents, and political party members, to prevent their being arrested, tortured, jailed, and executed. I was one of these people who had to go."

During this time, the young Javad had been studying dentistry at Tehran University Dental School, hoping for a career that would build him a good life. However, he found himself a political opponent of the new regime, and as soon he was able to finish dental school in 1986, he left Iran shortly afterward, seeking shelter, safety, and a fresh start in the United states. Thus, on June 1, 1986, Dr. Javad Ghoreishi arrived at Logan Airport in Boston, Massachusetts, his new home.

"I came here as an immigrant," he says, "Living as an immigrant in a new environment. It was very hard, but I obtained my green card based on my research."

That research, as it happens, was in the field of preventative dentistry and microbiology, and conducted nearby at the Forsyth (Institute) Dental Center, one of the most prestigious dental research facilities in the world: first founded in 1910 by Boston's Dr. Thomas Alexander Forsyth, today's Cambridge-located institute has grown to become of the world's leading centers for dental and craniofacial research, altogether. Back in 1986, though, in that same month wherein Dr. Javad was getting situated, he passed the first part of the National Dental Board, a written test which set him on the road to practice dentistry in the United States. Within his first year as a new immigrant, he passed two national boards. Two years later, while Dr. Javad was continuing to conduct dental research at the Forsyth Dental Center, he simultaneously began attending an Advanced Standing Program in Dentistry at Boston University Henry Goldman School of Graduate Dentistry (BUSGD). He graduated from this program in 1991.

The Forsyth Dental Center, as it happens, would prove to be a key chapter in Dr. Javad's life for a number of significant reasons – and not only in relation to the immigration process. For it was during these same studies, at that same center, where he first met a visiting dental clinician from Japan, named Aya Yakuza, and they began seeing one another. These two would, in the future, become married – tunneling deeper and deeper into a flawed, problematic relationship that never worked, for a variety of reasons – and leading to the dilemmas that Dr. Javad faces today.

Even in those early days of the relationship, Dr. Javad says, he had many reservations about Aya and his future, feeling strongly that her interest in him was more about a selfish desire for marriage, and the desire to not grow older without a husband and children. "She wanted to be married," he says, "But she did not want to be married to me." In the meantime, though, their paths were intertwined, both personally and professionally. And so, after Dr. Javad graduated from the Boston University Henry Goldman School of Graduate Dentistry, and following some time working in dental companies at Hollyhock and Worcester, he and Aya made the decision to start up a small dental office, shared between the two of them, in a condominium complex in Brookline Village. This decision, made in 1992, was made with the understanding of Dr. Javad's medical condition—which, since it was MS, would only worsen through the years—and the hope that their relationship would improve over time.

Needless to say, it didn't. And the story of why it didn't, and what went wrong over the years, runs parallel to the story of their dental practice itself.

2

A TROUBLED MARRIAGE

Today, when Dr. Javad Ghoreishi describes the marriage that would prove so destructive to his life, he speaks in frank terms.

"It was a highly mismatched marriage," he says. "We had no common ground. I handled the mismatched marriage, though, because I did not want my daughter to grow up without a father, but it was very hard."

While most divorcees can pinpoint the sharp, bladed corners where their marriage went wrong, Dr. Javad had a clear understanding about the inherent problems from the beginning, which had initially caused him some hesitation when Aya had increasingly pressured him for marriage, time and again. In the end, the reason he went for it was not due to his own enthusiasm, or any sort of blindness about the problems, but simply the hope that somehow, marriage might foster more shared understanding. As he tells it, "We had some cultural and sociopolitical differences that, to me, were a huge mismatch for what I had expected for my life. I was hoping marriage would bring our perspectives and insights closer to each other ... but later, after it ended, I see that marriage simply proved to me that this whole idea was the wrong conception." Her reasons, it seems, were far less hopeful, and rooted only in her own ego. "Later on," Dr. Javad says, "I realized that she only married me because, in her culture, being considered a 'spinster' is negatively regarded. It was only ever about her, not me, not us."

Javad's intuition would prove accurate. In essence, while so many marriages start out seeming wonderful and then take a painful downward spiral, the marriage between Dr. Javad and Aya seems to have started out in quite a bad place, and only gotten progressively worse as it went along. Just as so many problematic relationships grow inextricably worse and worse over the years, despite the problems, theirs did as well. Their problems were only exacerbated as their very careers became tightly interwound, even as the tension reached such a fever pitch that the two of them, while living in the same condominium, began living separate lives and never interacting with one another.

Before plunging further into these more intricate details, though, it is useful to jump back in time a bit, and survey the broad outline of the two dentists' lives together. After Dr. Javad and Aya started dating in school, she first moved in with him in 1988, and she graduated from Tufts Dental School in 1992. They married the following year, in 1993, and lived together in a one-bedroom condo in Watertown, Massachusetts. A couple years later, in 1995, they had their first and only child together—a daughter. That same year, they also purchased the three-bedroom condominium, in the same complex where their dental practice was. The downward spiral started speeding up at this point, as Dr. Javad recalls: "As soon as we moved to our new condominium, she separated her bedroom from me. It was the first sign of what was to come."

Now, an important factor in all of this, of course, is the matter of Dr. Javad's medical condition, which Aya was fully aware of at the time and throughout the entirety of their relationship, and which would go on to play a huge role in their divorce, years down the line. "I have a disease," Dr. Javad says. "MS. Multiple sclerosis. It is a disease which cannot be cured, and it has now left me wheelchair bound. She was aware of it the entire time. I took her everywhere, to show her my future."

Multiple sclerosis, as many readers are certainly aware, is an incurable condition. Impacting well over two million people globally, MS is actually the most common immune-mediated disorder affecting the central nervous system: as a demyelinating disease, it is known for damaging the nerve cells in the brain and spinal cord, which in turn causes an array of physical and psychological symptoms – such as muscle weakness, lack of coordination, blindness, the inability to walk, and so on – which may progressively worsen over time, as a person ages. Multiple sclerosis can have a devastating impact on the life of anyone it touches, from the person afflicted to the closest family members, and it is an equal-opportunity condition: there are many famous people who have been afflicted with MS, including Montel Williams, Jack Osbourne (the son of Ozzy Osbourne), Ann Romney (wife of Mitt Romney), and Selma Blair.

In addition, as an aging man with MS, Javad has survived other emergency situations that were compounded on by his condition.

In 2008, for example, he suffered from a heart Angiogram. He suffered from a fractured hip at one point, which necessitated an implant hip replacement. Today, his mobility is dependent upon a wheelchair, a motorized electric scooter, a special minivan, and the assistance of a caregiver for certain ADLs.

At this time, sadly, the true cause of MS is unclear, though it may be related to genetic and/or environmental factors, or perhaps some combination of the two. The name of the condition itself is a reference to the multiple sclerae (or lesions) which it causes to develop on the spinal cord and brain's white matter. Needless to say, multiple sclerosis is a painful and heart wrenching condition to be diagnosed with – physically, psychologically, and emotionally – and should be treated by a person's family members with the utmost kindness, understanding, and compassion, as well as using specialized methods to allow the disabled person to continue working, striving toward their goals, and accomplishing everything they want out of their life.

Kindness, understanding, and compassion, sadly, was not what Dr. Javad received from his wife Aya, who accommodated his condition only so far as it suited her own goals … which, as time went by, she made sure were clearly separated from his, for the most part. "She was always so negative toward my disability, the whole time," Dr. Javad says. "She was also very prejudiced. She knew what I had to go through but did not accept it. But yes, she knew the whole time." Currently, Dr. Javad uses a wheelchair to move around, but at the time he and Aya first began seeing each other, his condition had not yet declined to that point. Nonetheless, he was quite clear to her about where it *would* be going, in the future, and he was already at the point of using a cane to ambulate.

By 2001, Dr. Javad's MS had reached the point where he had to begin relying on a wheelchair for transportation. Being a studious person who was not afraid to look into the future and see what awaited him, Javad knew that he had to take action now, to ensure that he would be able to live as full a lifestyle as possible in the future, whenever his condition worsened further. In 2004, he modified their bathroom and shower area to accommodate his current condition, and to prepare for any future progressions. Meanwhile, as Dr. Javad was doing renovations to their condo to ensure independence in the wake of his declining medical condition, he also felt it was time to hire a personal care assistant (a PCA) to help him get ready for work in the mornings. While Dr. Javad was lucky enough at this time to have the means to hire a PCA himself, it's worth noting that doing so is not an abnormal response to the expected decline that occurs with MS. These PCAs, who often have experience working as CNAs (certified nursing aides) in settings such as nursing homes and rehab facilities, are uniquely trained, certified, and in some states licensed, to know the correct methods in which to transfer, bathe, and assist a disabled person to live as full a lifestyle as possible: in other words, their job is not to take away independence, but to ensure it.

Aya, from the beginning, was not happy about her husband choosing to hire a PCA. Looking at the full picture, though, Javad points out that her lack of understanding in this regard was not a huge surprise, because she showed him a shockingly low level of support for his condition throughout their marriage. One notable example of this can be seen by examining the way that Dr. Javad's condition required many medical visits and consultations, including two visits to a neurologist every year: while one would expect that Aya would have accompanied him to some of these, or at least been curious about them, he states that there was only one single time—over all those years—wherein Aya actually accompanied him to this neurologist. Even then, this particular visit came with a sharp caveat: Once there, it seemed, she had only come with him to ask the doctor if her husband might have been cognitively impaired, due to his condition. She was disappointed, evidently, to find out that he was *not* impaired. At this present time, Javad continues to have no cognitive impairment, despite the fact that various lawyers and other legal entities have attempted to slander him in this way.

In any case, this same sense of judgment, denial, and negativity was spotlighted in regard to Dr. Javad's decision in 2004 to hire PCAs to assist him with ADLs, or activities of daily living – essentially, because Aya sharply rejected the reality of his condition, and the needs that it presented. "She did not want to accept that my physical condition had changed," Dr. Javad says. "So, she kept treating my PCAs with disrespect, treating them so badly that after only a few days of working in our home, they would abruptly quit their job and leave." This presented a serious problem to Dr. Javad himself, because the mornings were the time that he most desperately needed this sort of physical assistance, which Aya was also not willing to provide to him. This put him in a rather desperate position, since having a reliable PCA would be necessary for him to have any semblance of an ordinary life, and she was driving all of them away in quick succession.

One male PCA, though, whom Dr. Javad refers to as Mr. Robinson, stuck with Dr. Javad through thick and thin, despite all of the mistreatment he faced from Aya. Dr. Javad first hired Mr. Robinson back in 2009, and he has continued using his services until the present day. As with so many strong caregiver/client connections, the friendship between Dr. Javad and Mr. Robinson is genuine, as opposed to simply being a business relationship. One moment that Dr. Javad remembers clearly – both because it showed Mr. Robinson's strength of character, as well as his wife's lack of concern for his well-being – occurred when Aya was on vacation in Machu Picchu. As she was away, the PCA came to Dr. Javad and admitted that he himself had experienced two divorces in his life, and this experience gave him the insight to see the deep cracks in Dr. Javad and Aya's marriage, as well. "As he saw the situation," Dr. Javad says, "He told me that she did not care for my well-being. In fact, he told me that she wanted me dead." In addition, Mr. Robinson informed Dr. Javad that Aya was trying to get him to leave Dr. Javad's employment, but assured him that he would not leave him, and would stay by his side to help him through any means necessary. Since then, Mr. Robinson has lived up to that promise, continuing to assist Dr. Javad seven days a week for over a decade. Over the years, Javad is lucky to have gained a second loyal and compassionate PCA, as well, named Venesha Aljoe. "I am very fortunate to have my PCAs," he says. "They are very good."

Still, going back to Mr. Robinson's insight: the truth in what he was saying, regarding Aya, deeply troubled Javad. It revealed to him what he already knew, deep down, which was that his wife would prefer for him to be out of the picture, as long as she was still able to benefit from him financially. This is, sadly, a situation that has ripped apart many families, as a successful family member who comes down with a disability, illness, or cognitive condition becomes nothing but a pile of dollar bills to greedy family members and/or spouses who forget to treat them as a human being. Still, Aya's utter disregard for Javad's condition was so thorough that Mr. Robinson was alarmed by it, which made it uniquely troubled, and perhaps highlighted the bigotry and money-grabbing that still lay ahead.

Meanwhile, as the growing tension in these marital problems tightened around Javad's throat like a noose, both he and Aya were working together. Dr. Javad describes this as being the worst life situation imaginable. "Think of there being an obvious problem between a married couple, like there was with both of us," he explains, "then imagine that you have them work at the same place, too. I had to put up with everything, draining me constantly, for our daughter's sake. Why? Because I grew up without a father, myself, which was very psychologically hard. I did not want my daughter to grow up the same way. So, I kept going, through the mistreatment she gave me, at home and at work. But it took a heavy toll on my well-being."

The setup and history of the dental practice itself, as it happens, would go on to become a key source of dispute in their future divorce, so it is important to detail all the work and time that Dr. Javad put into it, and to understand why not having it taken away from him – something that the courts and Aya's lawyer would later aggressively do, through illegal methods such a forgery – was so important for his career and livelihood to be intact.

The office, first purchased in 1992, was small in size (was 420 square feet, and later 1800 square feet) and, as previously mentioned, in the same complex as the condominium they called home. From the beginning, both of them were working at this office a full six days a week. This, of course, had to change when their daughter was born, since the baby required the full attention of at least one of them. To make this work, Aya took two months off. Once this maternity leave period was over, she reduced her working days to about two and a half days a week, in an attempt to balance both her profession and the needs that motherhood entailed.

In 1997 Dr. Javad bought the adjacent office unit that expanded the dental office to 1800 square feet, and he himself supervised the renovation of the new dental office to accommodate his disability. Dr. Javad never stopped working throughout this, of course, and his dental practice grew very profitable during the entire time, gaining loyal patients who appreciated his high level of skill, experience, and technique. "In my professional life, I became very successful," Dr. Javad explains. "Pedro Martinez, the Red Sox pitcher? He was my patient. I had a lot of famous, famous patients." This is significant, because for individuals such as Martinez, who have access to pretty much any dentist they could possibly ask for, Dr.

Javad was the one they chose. He proved himself, time and again, and truly distinguished himself within his profession.

Dr. Javad's scope of dental practice was quite large, and his duties in the office were no less thorough. He practiced all phases of dental procedures – root canals, surgical wisdom teeth extractions, gum surgery, crowns and bridges and surgical placement and restoration of dental implants – while simultaneously managing the practice itself, on a full-time basis. Due to his multiple sclerosis, and his foresight in regard to the challenges ahead, he also made the wise choice to have the entire office reconstructed in such a manner as to accommodate his disability. He managed this entire process from start to finish. That first meant getting permission from the condo complex's board of trustees, and curtailed into hiring and supervising plumbers, electricians, and other contractors to build and install dental chairs and other equipment, all of which he was the sole purchaser of. He also purchased all the hardware, the software, the computer supplies, the furniture, and other such needs, while simultaneously managing all contact with the electric company, the internet supplier, and more. He also solely purchased retirement benefits for his employees, purchased accountants for the office itself – he was the one who met with the accountant, to manage finances – and dental malpractice insurance companies for both he and Aya. Other tasks he performed for both Aya and himself included the regular renewing both of their dental X-ray licenses, renewing their dental licenses on a bi-yearly basis, and arranging for continuing education credits for both of them.

Obviously, this was a full plate. However, once the dental practice was established, he also made sure to take care of office duties such as interviewing and hiring employees, setting up payroll for each employee's biweekly check using ADP, and solely developing a database of addresses and phone numbers for both national and international health and dental insurance companies. Meanwhile, Dr. Javad was the one who solely purchased disability insurance for both he and his wife, verified that the dental office fully complied with state regulations and laws, and held weekly meetings with employees to hear any concerns and/or suggestions they might have. Dr. Javad filed an annual IRS form 5500 for each of the employees' 401K retirement accounts, and solely paid for all the business expenses and bills – while, at the same time, also paying for all the household expenses and bills.

Meanwhile, as Javad worked tirelessly to pay the expenses for the dental office, as well as the household expenses – Aya's income was only enough to pay her own dental office expenses, including an assistant—he was also paying for their daughter's private school education in Lexington, Massachusetts. As his daughter grew older, he bought her a one-bedroom condo: this was a matter that would grow complex after the divorce, when the judge awarded the condo to Aya, with instructions to manage it until their daughter graduated from college. That happened four years ago, yet to this day, the situation hasn't changed. " Aya still has a grip on my condo," Javad says, "Now, she rents it for enrichment, and the despot [the judge] ignored all my motions to give the condo to my daughter.

For now, though, going back to the marriage: All the money that Javad had to make, from top to bottom, required a lot of work. Work that was made more difficult by escalating tensions at home. However, Dr. Javad gained a loyal base of patients, and his credibility always showed through. "I established a very excellent reputation as a skilled dentist, and a community-oriented dentist." The importance of community, throughout his life, is something that he had always stressed immensely. Meanwhile, though, his physical health condition continued to decline, as it does with MS, and he believes that this was the primary factor in his wife's decision to file for divorce.

"When she saw that she was making more money, and would need to support me, due to my disease, she filed for divorce. And that was the beginning of another chapter in my life." Not a good chapter, though. As Dr. Javad puts it today, "During the divorce process I witnessed lies, racism, swindlers, deception, ignorance, and abuse of the position ... the system is racist."

Truthfully, as problematic as the marriage itself had been, the divorce would reveal itself to be a thousand times worse.

3

AN EVEN MORE TROUBLED DIVORCE

After the prejudice he has faced in the U.S. justice system, during his divorce trial, Dr. Javad Ghoreishi is understandably angry. Speaking on the matter today, he does not pull back any punches. "The justice system, as seen at the Norfolk Probate and Family Court, is completely racist," he explains. "The judges, the system, the treatment of people like me, all of it. The lawyers who I encountered are improper, crooked. Corrupt, except for Michael Traft. They lie, and the justice system is overloaded. The judges don't properly review the documents that are presented to the court. Then, I got a racist judge. He did not give me any credit, and he treated me as if I was less than human."

Before delving further into these later details, though, it is important to first rewind and get a strong sense of what went down at the beginning of the marriage's downward spiral, which turned this troubled marriage into a troubled divorce.

The pivotal event, as Dr. Javad sees it, was his hospitalization in 2008, due to the aforementioned heart angiogram. Before that point, while his MS had always been a factor, he had still been working tirelessly in the dental office, with a rate of high production and high earnings that allowed the family a very comfortable lifestyle, with no debt, and the realities of his health condition had yet to sink in. In 2008, though, when his heart condition required him to be rushed to the hospital, this was something that Aya, evidently, felt deeply troubled by. "After I was discharged from the hospital," Dr. Javad explains, "I told her that I had been working very hard, but that after this heart episode, I would like to reduce my workload, and that I would like her to engage more with the dental practice."

This was a game changer. Suddenly, it became clear to Aya that her husband's condition was a real thing that would only progressively worsen over the years, requiring her to step up her efforts instead of simply relying upon him. During this time, as well, Javad made what he now calls his "most horrific mistake," which was to change the billing information of the dental practice to her name. This would, indeed, come back to bite him following the initial divorce case, and result in legal battles that still continue to this day.

In any case, Aya's reaction to Dr. Javad's hospitalization, and his request for her to participate more in their shared dental practice, was not one of love, much less spousal support. "When she realized I could not be as productive as before," Dr. Javad says, "her attitude grossly changed toward me, and my life changed drastically."

Suddenly, after the scary medical incident Dr. Javad had survived – and his request for more help – he instead found that he had become *persona non grata* within his own home. "I was living and working like a single person," he says. "Each night, before opening the entrance door to my home, I rattled my keys, waited a few seconds, and would hear she and my daughter's footsteps as they ran to their rooms, hiding before I could enter." Dr. Javad says that it became normal for him to have to make his own dinner at night, after a long workday, and also to eat this dinner while no one was around. As traumatic as this situation sounds – hardly the portrait of a healthy home life – he says that this was the condition of their lives for three years. He accepted it as it was, even as it was clear that the cracks between the two of them were only progressively deepening.

Finally, in 2011, as Dr. Javad started doing research on medications for a patient, Aya filed for divorce.

Divorces in the United States are rarely a clean, friendly process. Even once-happy marriages can quickly spiral out into legal disasters, wherein one or both people are preyed upon by greedy legal professionals who try to decimate the other party, with little regard for the consequences this causes for the children. When you add in the oft-commented upon racial biases that run through the U.S. court system, as well as the streak of ableist prejudice against those with disabilities that Javad would soon learn about, the situation he entered was one in which every aspect of his career, past, and character would be torn apart, and soon, he would find even his ability to work and sleep at night being threatened. The stakes rose to heights he never could have anticipated beforehand.

This having been a particularly unhappy marriage, the process was rough at the very beginning, and worsened quite quickly. Right from the get-go, Aya Yakuza hired a law firm that, during the divorce process, Dr. Javad came to see as being established on forgery, deception, fabrication, and connections. The initial divorce filing came from one Elvira Adams—a person who would, later on, be forced to withdraw her application to be a justice due to issues at the troubled Probate and Family Court, as commented on by the news—and the lies and fabrication were there from the outset. As time went on, throughout the process, Javad was astonished and perplexed by the constant judgment he received from judges and lawyers, who constantly undermined or second-guessed his mental acuity.

When the divorce was first filed, at the time, Dr. Javad and Aya had agreed to split the working days of the dental office, 50-50, by having each dentist separately work there twelve days a month. This seemingly amicable arrangement, for the record, did not count the weekends: their arrangement, at this time, had Dr. Javad working every Saturday, with Aya only working on every other Saturday after the hour of 2:00 p.m. That changed quickly, without warning, and through a highly deceptive process. "To my consternation," Dr. Javad says, "During the divorce process, the law firm forged my signature on a document indicating that I have agreed to only work every other Saturday, which changed the working days to be unequal for me, toward her benefit. This would not be the last time my signature was forged, but it was the first sign of what awaited me."

Clearly, the divorce process was already off to a bad start, and it only got progressively worse, from there.

As Dr. Javad explains, "I told my counselor that I had not seen this document before, not once. This document had never been presented to me, for my signature. It was forged." To Dr. Javad's irritation, the counselor ignored this, and simply claimed that Dr. Javad had signed the document, even though he had not. "This wrong action from the other party, and the total inaction of my counselor, meant that I was forced to seek another counselor altogether."

Based on the recommendation of his dental assistant's father, Dr. Javad hired a new counselor named John Freeky. This would, sadly, prove to be a poor decision. According to Dr. Javad, Freeky was a deeply disturbing human being. "He himself told me that he travels to Thailand, or India, to have sex with underage girls," Javad says. Freeky would go on to misrepresent Javad, breach their contract, and effectively destroy his dental career – causing Dr. Javad to lose his dental office – following three days of trial, on July 8, 2013, due to the ruling of Judge Gestapo, a former military judge. Following John Freeky's inaction, Dr. Javad later would go on to bring a lawsuit against him, filing a complaint for a jury trial at Norfolk Superior Court. This cause was, ultimately, dismissed.

Going back to the divorce trial, though, Dr. Javad came away with a highly negative view of the judge, whom he describes as highly biased. "The egregious and insidious judgment that I received from the perfidious trial judge, consisted of 304 fictitious findings, made with bad faith tactics, corrupt motives, fraudulent calculations, and many, many lies, all within his findings and judgment. He also spoke many disparaging sentences toward me, clearly showing his prejudice against myself and others like me." Furthermore, Dr. Javad says that Judge Gestapo went out of his way to leave Dr. Javad financially decimated, to ruin his career, and put him the nearly impossible position of having to vacate his dental office within twenty days – which, recall, had been expensively redesigned to accommodate Dr. Javad's disability, thereby allowing him to continue his career without hardship – after which he was supposed to avoid the premises. This would have left Javad with no work to make additional income.

"Upon receiving Judge Gestapo's insidious judgment," Dr. Javad says, "it was … intense. Like shock therapy, it put me into deep distress. I felt distraught. I immediately sought to contest the judgment." Dr. Javad didn't know what to do, though, or where to turn to, and says that he found himself unable to focus or concentrate. Finally, he called his friend Ken, from Vermont, in a cry for help. Ken immediately responded by zipping right down to Massachusetts, staying with Dr. Javad for four days, and doing the necessary research to help him locate a new lawyer who could contest the previous judgment.

To start the process, Dr. Javad and Ken approached the problematic trial lawyer who had helped cause the situation, John Freeky, and asked him to obtain a stay order for the judgment, and to appeal it. Freeky refused. He claimed that he did not do appeals, and he told Dr. Javad to seek out an appellate lawyer for the job.

"He tried to wash his hands of the mess that he created for me. He is a cherry picker," Dr. Javad says.

Seeing how Freeky was not going to be of any use to his goals, he continued searching for a new appellate lawyer – preferably one who would actually do what he hired them to do. While also getting advice from another friend, a law student named Christopher, Dr. Javad kept hunting, until he finally came upon two lawyers who seemed like they could fit his needs, by the names of Ms. Trash, and Michael Traft. Javad was not sure which of them would necessarily be the better fit, so he interviewed both, and got the advice of Ken. Finally, after much thought, he decided that he would pick Ms. Trash.

Sadly, as Dr. Javad tells it, this would soon prove to be a terrible mistake.

4

VERMIN SWINDLERS

While Dr. Javad suffered through many painful and prejudiced circumstances throughout his divorce saga, his harshest words are reserved for the law partners of Ms. Trash and Mr. Garbage, a pair whom he refers to as "the vermin swindlers," and whose dishonest actions and exploitation of his disability were what first inspired him to write this very book. Dr. Javad explains that they used his condition to line their own pockets, through intimidation and lies – "As soon as they realized my medical situation, and my distress, they started ripping me off. That's why I call them vermin swindlers." And this was far from the only way he says that they took advantage of him.

Dr. Javad's first meeting with Ms. Trash and Mr. Garbage was at his own residence, due to the fact that her law firm was not handicap accessible. Ms. Trash was accompanied by another man, who introduced himself as Mr. Garbage, and explained that he was her husband. Mr. Garbage, evidently, was a criminal lawyer, and while he explained that he would not be involved with Dr. Javad's case, he preferred to always accompany his wife. This would become a point of contention, later on, as Mr. Garbage – despite claiming he wasn't representing Javad – would become inextricably bound in everything that was to come.

In any case, Dr. Javad and Ms. Trash discussed his case, with her having received a great deal of prior information about the details from his friend Ken. Ms. Trash told Dr. Javad, at this time, that Judge Gestapo had a reputation for being highly partial, and she referred to his judgment as a travesty of justice. This was, of course, what Javad had hoped to hear. In this meeting, Ms. Trash also stated that for the appeals process, she had to file a stay order to Judge Gestapo immediately: she explained that the judge would almost certainly deny this stay order, and once he did so, she would have to go to the Appeals Court, and file a stay order there. She also specified, as a plan going forward, that it was important for Dr. Javad to always be alone at home with her (and her husband) whenever she was doing his legal work. "I agreed to her plan," Dr. Javad says. "I did not realize the full extent of what I was agreeing to, because she hid many details." The key feature here, as well, was the demand for Javad to be alone. Looking at the situation from afar, this red flag was a small sign of what was to come in the near future.

The following day, both Ms. Trash and Mr. Garbage, returned to Dr. Javad's place, again doing so while he was alone, bringing a $25,000 contract for him to sign.

Even at this point, so early on in the process, some of the details seemed wonky, particularly in regard to the continual involvement of Mr. Garbage. While the husband had previously said he would not be involved with Dr. Javad's case, the contract contained a paragraph specifying that Mr. Garbage would be assisting Ms. Trash at the same hourly rate as her, but specified that this was "not duplicate." Understandably, Dr. Javad questioned this, trying to make sure he was only hiring Ms. Trash – and not both of them – and Mr. Garbage reassured Dr. Javad that he would not be working for Dr. Javad, but simply assisting his wife with the legal work. Iffy, to say the least, but once a contract has been presented before someone, particularly with a ticking clock in the background, it's hard to step away. They knew this. Javad did, as well, but at this point, he felt like he had to move quickly.

"In the devastating situation that I was in, and being in need of contesting the insidious judgment, I didn't have much room to argue," Dr. Javad says, looking back. "They both realized my desperate situation, and they told me that I had only six days left to obtain the stay order, so I signed the ambiguous contract, while I was all alone, without further counsel. Basically, they did not let me get advice. I felt I had no choice in the matter. Now, I see that hiring and signing a contract with Ms. Trash became an entirely new nightmare. Both she and her husband proved to be swindlers on a level beyond what I could have imagined." After this, the two lawyers returned the next day, whereupon they sat down with both Dr. Javad and Ken. Immediately, Ken wanted to make sure that Dr. Javad was not going to be swindled. "The very first question Ken asked Ms. Trash was to make sure that they would only be billing me for one lawyer, since it was always her and her husband arriving. And, in response, Ms. Trash deceived him."

According to the contract, as written, Dr. Javad was obligated to pay the $25,000 in contract fees in three sections, with the first section, for $10,000, required early on as a fee for initiating the process. The second strange thing that occurred, however, was the way that Ms. Trash and Mr. Garbage went about obtaining this first payment, by barging into Dr. Javad's home – in a fifteen-story apartment building – unannounced, without warning, and forcing their way in. When Dr. Javad asked how they had managed to get inside the building, they simply responded that someone had left the door open. As it happens, this would grow to become a habit of theirs.

They asked for the first payment. Dr. Javad wrote a check for the desired amount. Ms. Trash looked at it, handed it back, and said that his handwriting was not acceptable: she demanded that she be allowed to write the check herself, and then she would have him sign it for authentication. Strange as this sounded, Ms. Trash swiftly made this a rule in their relationship, stating that if at any point Dr. Javad did not follow this rule, she would not do the required work on his case – knowing, of course, that she'd pulled him into a scenario where he now held no other option except to follow her orders. The same process, with her writing the check and him signing it, would continue for the second and third payments. "I had to sign these checks, under their pressure, to save myself from having a heart attack."

Meanwhile, other deceptive practices soon went into action. On the last day that Dr. Javad had left before the judgment for him to evacuate his dental office was to take effect, Ms. Trash and Mr.

Garbage arrived at his home with a sunflower, a bottle of wine, and the big news that she had been able to obtain a temporary stay order from the Appellate Court, meaning Dr. Javad wouldn't have to lost his dental office the following day. Now, on the surface, this was great news, and that's how Dr. Javad took it at the time. In the midst of this celebration, he never thought to ask for more details. "I was so very happy, so overwhelmed with the happiness of getting to stay in my dental office, that it prevented me from asking Ms. Trash the real question – on what basis did she obtain the stay order, and how?"

That, as it happened, was a matter of deep concern. Some weeks later, the couple returned to Dr. Javad's residence, once again unannounced, with a letter from the Appellate Court explaining that the single judge who had rendered the temporary stay order had now referred Dr. Javad to the same judge as before – Judge Gestapo – and that Dr. Javad now had a mere three days to prove that his disability required him to stay in the same dental office, rather than working in a different one. He was back in the same situation as before, but with an even tighter deadline. Gestapo's order clearly ignored the fact that Dr. Javad's office had been specifically renovated for the sake of accommodating his disability, as well as the obvious fact that most dental offices are not renovated in this manner, leaving Dr. Javad in a highly vulnerable and precarious position, desperate and unsure of where to turn. It was in that exact state of panic, it seems, that Ms. Trash and Mr. Garbage continued to take full advantage of Dr. Javad's uncertainty: on that Friday afternoon, knowing that his court date was the coming

Monday, giving him no time to think, prepare, or find anyone else, they swept in and demanded more money than had been agreed to previously. "She gave me a bill for $65,446. I didn't even look at the bill. Mr. Garbage took my checkbook and wrote a check for $40,446, payable to them, and he said to me that if I did not sign the check, Ms. Trash would not represent me anymore, and would not go to the coming court session."

As a disabled person, Javad was forcibly intimidated by their presence within his home, using his materials, telling him what to do. He had only a weekend to make something happen. They were his only lawyers. He'd been put in a box, lied to, and didn't feel like he had a choice but to proceed further. "My biggest fear was facing the perfidious judge, and they were aware of the fact that, firstly, I am alone, and it is hard for me to make a wise and rational decision. They used my disability against me. So, they did not leave me with any other option, but to sign the check written by Mr. Garbage."

So, Javad agreed, under duress, to letting them write themselves a check from his pocket. The weekend passed. Monday arrived. To Dr. Javad's surprise, when he arrived at the Family and Probate court, he saw not Ms. Trash, but Mr. Garbage. "He told me Ms. Trash would be coming soon," Dr. Javad says. Dr. Javad entered the courtroom, followed by Mr. Garbage, and Ms. Trash finally arrived some minutes afterward. Aya's counselor came over with some paperwork for Ms. Trash, which the lawyer looked at and assessed without briefing Dr. Javad about their contents.

The court session proceeded, and the couple represented Dr. Javad. Once it was over, everyone parted ways, and Dr. Javad returned home – only to be shocked by what he found on the bill that Ms. Trash and Mr. Garbage. "So much of it was fictitious," he says. "Many of the working hours were duplicated, creating sixteen-hour workdays on different days." Meanwhile, the couple continued applying the same tactics to Dr. Javad – he says that, at this point, they saw him as a "goldmine" – and continually showing up at his place unannounced, barging in, and crafting detailed justifications for why Dr. Javad needed to continue paying them more money One incident, involving Aya's counselor being an insider, led the couple to demand another $15,000 from Dr. Javad, at which point Mr. Garbage took Dr. Javad's checkbook, and wrote themselves a check for $7,000. "I signed this only because I feared for my life," Dr. Javad explains. "I was alone, they were in my home, so much was on the line. I did not know what else to do, they were standing right there, and so I signed."

This was not the end of the fiasco. Two days later, Ms. Trash and Mr. Garbage returned to Dr. Javad's home, demanding another payment. Dr. Javad had only $6,000 left in his bank account, which he explained to them, but they would not leave without accepting another payment, so Garbage proceeded to once again take Dr. Javad's checkbook, this time writing a check for $3,000, which he then presented to Dr. Javad to sign. "They stood behind me, telling me to sign. Again, I feared for my life. I forced myself to sign the check to them."

This time, though, after they left, Dr. Javad did not accept the perilous status quo—it was clear, by now, that the couple was only going to continue demanding money from him—and he took action. "As they left my home, I waited for a while to make sure they were not coming back. Then, I went to the Brookline Police Department."

Sadly, the legal system is built to protect itself, rather than the innocent victims who are wronged by it, and in this instance, the police department did not do much to soothe Dr. Javad's fears and tension. After explaining his story to the officer, regarding the treatment that the lawyers were putting him through and the fear he felt for his life, the policeman said that there was nothing he could do. The only advice he offered was that if they returned, and if Dr. Javad again felt his life was in danger, he could call the Brookline Police Department and they would arrive. This was hardly any reassurance, considering that Dr. Javad was a disabled person being threatened by powerful, able-bodied individuals, pressuring him through both psychological and physical intimidation. What if they did not allow him to make the phone call? Even if the police did arrive, would they believe what Javad told them? He was in a truly precarious position, as the lawyers saw fit to barge into his home at any time, and continually bully him into spending increasingly exorbitant amounts of money.

Meanwhile, the court cases continued, as Aya came with a new counselor attorney, named Al Capone, who would prove to be deeply problematic later on. Dr. Javad continued to be represented by Ms. Trash and Mr. Garbage. On October 29, 2013, Judge Gestapo denied the temporary stay order that had previously been granted by the Appeals Court: this meant that after everything that had happened, Dr. Javad was still forced to vacate from his dental office, rendering him unable to work, until the Appeals Court made a permanent decision regarding the office.

One week later, the "vermin swindlers" knocked on Dr. Javad's door again. "They came into my home with happy faces, as usual, and told me they had received a contempt complaint from Al Capone, Aya's attorney, stating that I was not in compliance with the court order, even though I was in compliance of the judge's egregious order. Al Capone, knowing the fact that the perfidious judge was against me, filed a falsified contempt complaint against me."

Disturbing as this news may have been, the situation got even more complicated, very quickly. Right there and then, as Dr. Javad and the two lawyers were sitting in his living room, he heard the doorbell ring. He answered it, and he found himself face-to-face with a man claiming to be a constable, who asked to verify his identity as Dr. Javad Ghoreishi. Javad, of course, affirmed this was the case, and received a letter, which he opened as the constable left: inside the envelope was a court summons, and a short motion for contempt, with a request for $5,000 worth of lawyer fees.

By this point, remember: the law firm of Ms. Trash and Mr. Garbage had already bled Dr. Javad utterly dry, demanding money and resources that he barely had, and failing to rescue him from being exiled from the dental office he required in order to do his work. However, the lawyers seated there showed no sympathy for Dr. Javad's plight, and instead, simply demanded more money. Dr. Javad says that immediately said that this contempt situation was a brand "new case," and so she demanded that he cough up an additional $30,000 if he wanted her and Mr. Garbage to represent him in court. Dr. Javad told them, quite bluntly, that he was out of cash, and could not do that. "I was realizing that these vermin swindlers were really thinking they had discovered a goldmine, and taking full advantage of me," he reflects. "Remember, in just two months, they had collected $75,445 for themselves. Now they wanted another $30,000 for a contempt case. I told them I did not have more money to give them. My mistake was to mention that I did have money in my 401K account, that can be cashed to pay them the money."

The lawyers saw an opportunity to further bully him, and thus, they told him to call up his 401K account that very moment. "So, I called the AXA retirement company, and told them that I wanted to cash out my retirement money. Over the phone, I was told they would email me the forms, which I would need to fax back to them." Mr. Garbage, at this point, interjected to say that Dr. Javad should ask them if they could send him a check overnight: in response, AXA said that to do so, a credit card payment would be required. A few minutes later, Dr. Javad received the forms via email. He printed them, by the instruction of Mr. Garbage, who then said he would fill the forms out for Dr. Javad, and simply request his signature at the end.

"I stared at them as they filled out these forms. I saw greed on their faces and money in their eyes."

Once Ms. Trash and Mr. Garbage had finished filling out the document, Dr. Javad informed them that the only way he could send them was through fax, and that he would have his helper use the fax machine when she came back to work. Mr. Garbage sharply reminded Dr. Javad that he should put a credit card number down for overnight delivery, as if to ensure that they would get Javad's money in their pockets as soon as possible, and said to call him as soon as the fax was sent.

Javad had other plans. He'd seen what was happening, and was ready for it to stop. "Once the vermin swindlers had left my home," Dr. Javad details, "I called the attorney Michael Traft, the man I first considered before regrettably choosing Ms. Trash. On the phone, I asked Michael Traft if he remembered my case. He did. Then, I asked if he was willing to take over my appeals case, and contest the judgment on my behalf, instead of me continuing to do business with the vermin swindlers." To Dr. Javad's relief, Traft agreed to do so. Dr. Javad was also pleased to hear that Traft's office was wheelchair accessible, so they agreed for him to visit him there once the phone call was over.

By the time Dr. Javad arrived at the office, Traft had already prepared a contract for him to sign. From the outset, this experience was proving like night and day compared to what he had gone through with Ms. Trash and Mr. Garbage. "To me, contrary to the approach of the vermin swindlers, Traft's approach toward me – the whole way he explained the case, and described Judge Gestapo – he seemed like a true professional. And he continued to be that way, all through." Impressed, Dr. Javad made arrangements with Traft for the upcoming contempt case, and he hired him on the spot.

Now that Dr. Javad's new course was set, though, he now had the difficult task of cutting ties with the previous lawyers who had cheated him in such a vulgar fashion. One day after meeting with Traft, Ms. Trash called Dr. Javad's phone. He didn't answer, and she left voicemail, telling him to call her back immediately. After some time, and no response, she emailed him with a similar message, asking him to send confirmation that he had faxed the document to the retirement company. This time, Dr. Javad did respond, by bluntly telling her that she would no longer be representing him, and he had hired another lawyer to continue his case in her place. "I wrote to her that Ms. Trash and Mr. Garbage were after my money only, and nothing else."

Ms. Trash didn't take long to reply. She disputed Dr. Javad's argument – expressing surprise at his action, since she allegedly had perceived him as being happy with her service – and stating that his impression was wrong, and that she had only demanded the $30,000 because it was necessary for the work that had to be done. Her email, which was long and wordy, attempted to paint Javad as being a cognitively disabled person who was making empty accusations about her, as if she and her husband had been the victims of the situation. Of course, she did not admit to any wrongdoing.

While waiting for the Appeals Court decision, Dr. Javad was alarmed to discover that two of the contested properties, both of which were debt-free – the much-discussed dental office condominium, and the residential condominium – had been secretly and illegally transferred to the ownership of Aya Yakuza, without his knowledge or consent, in a form notarized by her attorney, Al Capone.

This revelation came about after a visit to the Brookline town hall, where Dr. Javad had gone to find out why he had not received property tax information, since he had generally paid these in person before that point. Once he discovered this information, Dr. Javad was advised to go to the town assessor office, located on the third floor of the same building, which he did. After explaining his situation there, from his past history of paying the property tax to the nightmare that had become his divorce case, the town assessor presented two deeds in hand, which showed Dr. Javad allegedly signing the properties over to Aya with, as previously mentioned, her attorney as the notary. Dr. Javad, having never seen these forms before and certainly not signed them, was flabbergasted, and immediately phoned up Michael Traft. Taft initially believed that this wrongdoing must have occurred before he had begun to represent Dr. Javad, but upon finding that it was more recent, he told Dr. Javad that he would call Al Capone, and try to get to the bottom of the matter.

Remember, this was the second time Javad's signature had been illegally forged, during this process.

Some days later, Traft called back. Evidently, Al Capone was claiming that the deeds had been drafted at his law firm, and he'd notarized them without reading them. Dr. Javad, terrified to be living in a home that was threatening to rip away from him at any moment, could only wait a few days for both lawyers to get back to him. "My biggest fear, at the time, was that I would be forced to vacate my home. The judgment had been crafted to decimate me, favoring a vicious party … and later, that viciousness would clearly be illuminated, even further." Looking at the situation, from afar, it's hard to even picture just the level of pain and anxiety that Dr. Javad must have been going through, as a disabled person with a worsening medical condition, having had all of his money swindled away from him … and soon, if the right moves weren't made, no home to call his own, unable to make income either through his practice or through selling the property.

The situation was dire. Dr. Javad had no choice but to act fast. So, to get into the process of taking his home back, he took a trip down to the Boston Overseers Organization, or BBO, to complain about the forged deed documents. "As soon as I showed the judgment, and the illegally conveyed deeds, to the BBO, the officer agreed to take action on this issue. He gave me a BBO complaint against lawyers form, and he advised me to fill the form, and a briefing of my discoveries." While Dr. Javad informed the officer that he had also reported the wrongdoing to the local attorney general, the officer told him that this was a waste of time, as the only action they would take would be to refer him back to the BBO, where he was already. This nugget of advice proved to be accurate.

Approximately two weeks later, after having mailed the complaint form back to the BBO, Michael Traft phoned up Dr. Javad, and asked him to go to his office so he could sign the new, correct deed, and put this particularly scary matter behind him, at least for the time being. Dr. Javad did go there the following day, accompanied by his friend Mohammad Kochak, and signed the two corrected deeds, for both the office and the residence condominiums. While doing this, Dr. Javad did make a point to ask Traft if signing the deed would get in the way of his Appeals Case, since ideally the property would soon no longer be shared with Aya Yakuza, and Traft responded affirmatively.

At this point, having ensured his own safety and well-being in regard to having his property back, Dr. Javad was ready to start taking legal action against the lawyer who had nearly robbed him of a home. "I did not want this wrong action by attorney Al Capone to go unnoticed. I did not want him to get away with it. So, I went to the Brookline Police Department, to report the forgery."

While a police officer took down Dr. Javad's report, and things seemed to be moving smoothly, the process hit a roadblock a few days later, when the department mailed Dr. Javad to inform him that since the forgery had, evidently, not happened within the city limits of Brookline itself, he would have to pursue further action in whatever place where the forgery did occur. Despite this setback being rather disappointing, Dr. Javad did what the letter specified, and he went to the Norfolk Family and Probate Court. However, after telling of his hardships to the clerk, she responded by stating that this was a divorce court, and did not handle the matter of forgeries, so he would have to bring his case to the Canton Police.

Still undeterred by the obstacles repeatedly being put in his path, Dr. Javad proceeded to the offices of the Canton Police Department, to repeat his story once more. Fortunately, he didn't have to wait as long, this time, before someone responded. "Fortunately," Dr. Javad says, "while I was waiting for the officer to come and speak with me, Canton's chief of police came to the waiting room, saw me on my wheelchair, and asked why I was there. I told him my whole divorce story, as well as the details of the forgery case. He listened very well."

As Dr. Javad was explaining these details, another officer joined the conversation and listened just as intently. At the end, this officer commented with empathy, stating that the lawyers were clearly "crooked." Following this, the Chief asked Dr. Javad what sort of outcome he expected from all of this, and Dr. Javad responded that he wanted to see the vermin swindlers put in jail. While empathetic to Dr. Javad's situation, the chief laughed at this, and expressed the unfortunate reality that this was an unrealistic assumption: as the chief put it, the most likely outcome was merely a slap on the wrist from the judge. Dr. Javad, accepting this, replied that "At least their licenses should be revoked." The chief said that even this hope was optimistic. However, he asked Dr. Javad to remain in the waiting room while he worked on some details, to try to help him. When he returned, he said that he had called the Brookline Police Department's chief, and that they would – at the very least – make arrangements for the forgery case.

This was, finally, after everything that Dr. Javad had suffered, a step in the right direction, and he was thankful. While the matter of the divorce and property disputes were still up in the air, at least this was a good sign of progress on the forgery case. Even better, when Dr. Javad returned home later that day, he was called by Brookline's Chief of Police, and thanks to the other Chief's call, he now had an appointment scheduled to talk to a detective, who would be handling the forgery case from that point forward.

The discussion with the detective, when it occurred, seemed positive enough – at first. The detective explained that he was going to have all the parties involved with the forgery case interviewed, and these interviews would be recorded on film. Following this, Dr. Javad would be notified of the results, whatever they might be. A few days later, though, Dr. Javad did receive a report from the detective. The conclusion? That the forgery had not occurred in Brookline – a fact that had already been known beforehand, and which barely moved the needle forward on Javad's goal.

In response to this, Dr. Javad made his return to the Canton Police Department, with the Brookline police report in hand. Canton's police officers, following what he asked, did some telephone interviews with both Michael Taft and Al Capone. The Canton Police Department then proceeded to craft their own report, but this ended in the same infuriating manner, as their "conclusion," as it were, was that the forgery had not occurred in Canton.

At this point, Dr. Javad was no longer sure how to proceed, so he asked the police for advice on his next step. The only thing that the officer could suggest, in this regard, was that Dr. Javad had the right to take both his ex-wife and her dishonest attorney before a judge, using the police reports as evidence of wrongdoing. Basically, he had to advocate for himself, do all the work himself, and hope that these minimal reports somehow helped him achieve the results that he sought.

Now, at this point, it's important to keep in mind that while the forgery case swallowed up a massive amount of time, Dr. Javad was simultaneously having to balance multiple cases, all of them the result of poor and/or dishonest representation, the biases in the court system, and the sheer difficulty he faced as a disabled person being taken advantage of by so many legal parties and entities. Keep in mind, that amidst all of this, Javad also had to pursue justice against the "vermin swindlers" of Ms. Trash and Mr. Garbage, pointing out that not only had they been acting outside of their area of expertise – and producing poor results, while demanding more money from him, a clear breach of ethics – but that they had also, using his physical disability to their advantage, intimidated him into writing checks, a violation of his rights. Trash disputed his account of events.

Looking back, though, it became clear to Dr. Javad that the start of his problems, on a legal level, were rooted in the representation he received from John Freeky, back at the beginning of this fiasco. By law, Dr. Javad had only three years to bring charges against Freeky after first hiring him, and so, he brought the lawsuit forth in December of 2015.

The lawsuit was brought to the Norfolk Superior Court. Dr. Javad specifically requested that he would like to have a jury trial, in case his case could be dismissed beforehand. Dr. Javad deposed Freeky himself, and in his deposition he attested to the partiality of Judge Gestapo and his 304 fictitious findings. His case at the Norfolk Superior Court was initially heard by the first judge, and finally, the case was dismissed by another judge. This dismissal was because, according to the latter judge, Dr. Javad had not thought to bring forward a witness, despite having ample time to do so. In fact, Dr. Javad – not possessing a legal background – had simply not known he would be required to name a witness before the jury trial, since he was not aware of the procedures of said jury trial. He had, from the start, intended to use his lawyer Michael Traft as a witness, but when he tried to bring Traft forward in an emergency motion, Freeky's attorney opposed it, on the grounds that Traft was an Appeals lawyer himself. By this point, Javad did not have time to find a replacement witness.

"In the judicial system, these judges used to be lawyers themselves," Dr. Javad points out. "Because of that, they never rule against another lawyer, and so, the John Freeky case was dismissed, without ever making it to a jury trial." Because of this, Dr. Javad's case was dismissed on a technicality. Dr. Javad – as an immigrant, and a disabled person, with no background in law – had been at a disadvantage from the outset in regard to forcing the lawyer who had wronged him to face real consequences, and the judge had shown him no sympathy. The system had won.

However, Dr. Javad didn't give up. That wasn't in his nature, and he had other massive legal battles ahead of him ... particularly in regard to his wife's new lawyer, Al Capone, who would prove just as problematic and prejudiced as the "vermin swindlers" had been, if not more so. As time went on, and the situation became messier, Javad would bring charges against Aya and Capone: at the time of this writing, this litigation is still ongoing at the Suffolk Superior Court.

5

OCEANS OF MOTIONS

O n March 7, 2016, Dr. Javad Ghoreishi finally received the decision of the Appeals Court.

Their conclusion was disappointing, to say the least. "The insidious judgment was so grotesque and outrageous that they did not even publish their decision," Dr. Javad explains, "and remanded the case for redivision of marital property, including my dental office, for retrial by a different judge at the Norfolk Probate and Family Court. "Looking at my struggle to have a fair retrial at the troubled Norfolk Probate and Family Court, I came to the sad realization that if my first vacated trial was a tragedy ... well, the second trial remand in this court was going to be a farce. A travesty of justice, you could say ... That is exactly what happened."

Ask any non-lawyer who has ever struggled with the perils of the U.S. court system, and you will hear the infamous truth about how lengthy, protracted, and exhausting the whole process really is. This is not just a stereotype, but an unfortunate reality. Dr. Javad had already learned as much, of course, through his prior legal battles, but now, he faced a new level of withdrawn stretching.

"The troubled Norfolk Probate and Family Court applied its utmost power to procrastinating the remanded case for retrial, as by violating the basic principles of law, in many conceivable ways, it could delay the remand retrial."

The case finally went to trial, with more than 260 different motions and subpoenas – as Dr. Javad tells it, "oceans of motions" – and at the cost of over nine years of utterly exhausting struggle for Dr. Javad Ghoreishi himself, who had to balance multiple cases, his health issues, new financial concerns, and the anxiety of the looming decisions, all at the same time.

Meanwhile, jumping sideways, other stuff was happening prior to the Appeal Court's decision. When it came to the divorce case, which had launched all the insanity to begin with, it was now brought before another judge at the Norfolk Probate and Family Court. By this time, Dr. Javad's ex-wife had decided to move onto a new lawyer, and hired Herman Goring, who Dr. Javad describes quite negatively. "He has a pernicious mind. Going into this trial, Goring was ready to rely heavily on his clout in the judicial system, feeling he could get away with anything in the troubled Norfolk Probate and Family Court. He openly lied to me and the judge, many many times, with actual malice … basically, he proved he was willing to do anything for money."

Dr. Javad goes so far as to accuse this lawyer of doing actions that "even rats would not do. For one, he contrived and wrote a motion to take me before the perfidious judge Gestapo, in which my refusal to appear before the judge, caused him to fail to prevail." Following this, Dr. Javad explains that Herman Goring filed yet another motion, based on the prior judgment, and when he took Dr. Javad before Judge Clawn, Dr. Javad was forced to not only pay money to the other party, but due to the extreme partiality of the judge, had to award attorney fees to Goring, as well. This was a devastating loss.

Herman Goring, however – and despite all the damage he had already done – was not finished tearing Dr. Javad down, yet. "Right after his big victory, Herman Goring wrote another bogus motion, and once again took me before Clawn." This motion, though, was denied by Clawn.

After the case remanded to the Norfolk Probate and Family Court, Dr. Javad got some assistance from his attorney, Michael Taft, who wrote a motion for him to get his office back before the remand trial. This motion was taken to Judge Clawn, who denied it. A pretrial conference with Clawn had produced no results.

Now, this brings the matter back to Herman Goring, a lawyer who not only did not care about Dr. Javad's disability, but in flagrant disregard for the man's well-being – and with utmost prejudice and ableism – tried to use that disability against him, for the sake of winning.

First off, it's important to know that in the United States, disabled persons are supposed to be protected by the Americans with Disabilities Act of 1990, also called ADA, which was a civil rights law that legally prohibited discrimination based on a person's disability, and also requires employers to provide "reasonable accommodations" to employees with disabilities, as well as requiring public locations to allow disabled access. For the non-disabled person, this language is mainly just something a person recognizes as the small text they tune out when applying for a job, or which is generally tacked to a bulletin board in the break room. For landlords, it's a major factor they have to consider. And most importantly, for disabled persons themselves, the ADA is supposed to be a lifeline, which allegedly ensures that they will receive full, equal treatment, before the law, and never see their disability used to bludgeon them, or prevent them from having the equal rights they deserve.

This, sadly, was not Dr. Javad's experience.

Herman Goring, Dr. Javad explains, used his clout to directly refute the Americans with Disabilities Act, and to force Dr. Javad out of the disputed office, and the dental profession altogether. Evidently, Goring wrote a letter to the Massachusetts Board of Registration In Dentistry, and tried to get them to discipline his dental license, on the ground that his physical disability prevented him from doing his work safely. This was, of course, total nonsense: Dr. Javad had been safely practicing dentistry for years, even on famous and wealthy patients, and his only requirement was for the office to be structured in a way that accommodated his disability. Herman Goring was out for blood, though, and he was willing to destroy Dr. Javad's entire reputation, career, and source of income to get it.

Looking more closely at the matter, though, it seems that Goring's toxic prejudices against disabled people ran deeper than just this one case. In several emails to Michael Traft, Herman Goring referred to Dr. Javad as "an old dog who belongs in a junkyard," and argued that his physical disability, due to MS, rendered him a "danger to society." In an effort to push out the remand trial, contrary to the Appeals Court decision, Herman Goring wrote a bogus motion claiming that Dr. Javad's disability was the central issue of the remand case for retrial. "And Judge Clawn," Dr. Javad says, "to my perplexity, allowed Herman Goring's motion. The partiality of Judge Clawn was so great that he allowed this to occur, contrary to the ADA and the Appeals Court decision."

Dr. Javad made the fateful decision to represent himself. "Herman Goring's misconduct and misbehavior, and the partiality of the judges of the troubled Norfolk Probate and Family Court, made me study and learn litigation law, and family law, in addition to the jurisprudence that I had to learn at the dental school."

Despite not being a lawyer, he had some experience to draw on, at the very least. "I previously learned to litigate attorney John Freeky, and attorneys Ms. Trash and Mr. Garbage, and so I litigated Herman Goring at Norfolk Superior Court. Later, I transferred the case to Suffolk Superior Court."

This case was dismissed. The reason? Supposedly, Herman Goring, despite the horrible nature of his actions in direct refutation of the ADA, apparently had absolute immunity in defense of his client, allowing him to take any legal action. If there was one positive from this whole ordeal, though, it was that Judge Christine M. Roach ruled that Herman Goring was in violation of a lawyer's professional conduct.

This story, though, was not yet over. More problems lay ahead.

6

REMAND RETRIAL

Throughout all of these many struggles that Dr. Javad Ghoreishi faced in the hostile and prejudiced world of U.S. courtrooms, he always found himself pitted against problems far larger than himself. Bias, both implicit and explicit, was wound through every case. Judges and lawyers treated him differently than they would a more privileged person, and they thought less of him, due to his disability and his place of origin. Through every step of the way, greedy figures tried to rip him to pieces in the hope of lining their pocketbooks with more dollars. Dr. Javad, though, has continued striving to see justice delivered to those who have abused the principles of the law.

"I fight back," he says. "And I have the intelligence to learn, and to deliver."

This would be proven, time and again, through every twist in the road. Somewhere around the month of May 2016, Judge Clawn – who, at this time, was planning to retire within the next year – made it clear that the remand case, within the halls of the Norfolk Probate and Family Courtroom, would take a long time to actually go to trial. He announced in the courtroom itself that the court would use any and all conceivable means to keep the retrial case lingering as long as possible. As Javad tells it, Clawn himself "entertained" the remand case until the point where he had retired, thereby meaning that all of Javad's waiting had been for nothing.

From here, the remand case was transferred to another judge in the Norfolk Probate and Family Court, named Judge Harrison. From the outset, though, it was clear that Judge Harrison's involvement in the case posed a severe conflict of interest: in her first session, she revealed that she had previously worked with Aya's counselor, Herman Goring. To her credit, she immediately withdrew herself from the case.

From here, the case landed in the lap of yet another judge at the same court – this time, Judge Ward. To Dr. Javad's deep irritation, though, the delays continued in exactly the same way as they had been doing before. "Judge Ward entertained the retrial case for almost a year, until she was transferred to another Family and Probate court." Once again, the case had stalled out to judicial inactivity, and a new judge needed to be found. It was a truly exhausting process, which required constant activity on Javad's part, to ensure that the case did not simply slip through the cracks. "While I was going to the troubled Norfolk Probate and Family Court, I made it clear to them, quite certainly, that I was not going to give up pursuing justice for my remand case, no matter what dirty game they played, in their efforts to discourage me." After everything Dr. Javad had suffered through, from the vermin swindling of Ms. Trash and Mr. Garbage to the outright prejudice of Herman Goring, Dr. Javad had no intentions of stepping back, no matter how drained he might have felt. He was willing to do whatever it took to right the wrongs perpetrated by the lawyers, and to try to have their ability to practice law – and to abuse others, like he had been abused – removed from them.

In the end, there would prove to be five judges that would be assigned to the case. "I appeared before four judges, in my efforts to try to get a fair retrial, based on the Appeals Court's decision. Finally, in the summer of 2018, I went back to the Appeals Court and told them the story." This time, though, when Dr. Javad explained his years of struggle to an Appeals Court clerk – and once the details had been verified – Dr. Javad says that the clerk was "flabbergasted," and claimed that in all of his seventeen years working at the Appeals Court, he had never seen anything like this happen.

The clerk advised Dr. Javad to go back to the Norfolk Family and Probate Court, pen in hand, and write an expedited motion for retrial of the remand case. On the following day, never backing down, Dr. Javad did exactly this. The clerk's office, here, sent him to a new judge's courtroom.

While Dr. Javad was waiting to be called by the judge, a court clerk tapped Dr. Javad on the shoulder, and asked him to follow her out of the courtroom. He did as she asked, and he was then directed to go to another courtroom, where he would see Judge Despot, a judge who had evidently never worked with the lawyer Herman Goring.

A reminder: by this point, it was the middle of July, 2018. Already, more than two years had passed since the remand case for retrial. Seven years had passed since Aya had initially filed for divorce. These drawn out, racist, and confusing legal battles had swallowed up almost the entirety of Dr. Javad's life for over half a decade, and even still, he was having to go out of his way to seek justice for the ways in which he was wronged. It's also worth remembering that, throughout this entire terrible process wherein Dr. Javad's case had been bounced from judge to judge over and over, he had to write dozens of subpoenas, motions, pretrial memorandums, and more, all of which did nothing to produce results.

However, flashing back ahead to that day in the summer, Dr. Javad followed the clerk's advice, and he entered the courtroom of Judge Despot. Sadly, Despot would prove just as problematic as the previous judges had been, but in a different way.

"By the way this judge handled the remand case," Dr. Javad details, "I … it is hard to find the proper description, but I know despots, from back in Iran. And this judge was a despot."

The following September of 2018, Dr. Javad and his attorney Michael Traft appeared before Judge Despot, in a session wherein Despot was scheduled to hear three motions. That did not occur. Despot not only completely ignored the motions, but also took away Dr. Javad's ability to speak for himself. "The despot turned off the court microphones. When I tried to speak, with it off, I could not speak out about the scheduled motion that he had ignored."

Dr. Javad, aghast at what was happening, fought back. He responded to these actions by writing a new motion, asking Judge

Despot to recuse himself from the case, on the basis of prejudice and bias. "The despot did not even address my motion," Dr. Javad relates. "He ignored the motion. Completely."

Still, Dr. Javad didn't give up: " I wrote another motion, arguing that Herman Goring was in violation of a lawyer's professional conduct, basing this on Judge Roche's ruling at Boston Superior Court. The despot did not address this motion, and ignored it, too."

Dr. Javad kept pushing, as he had previously pushed against so much corruption in the past. He wrote a complaint letter to the Commission on Judicial Conduct, arguing that the Judge Despot had acted in bad faith. "Instead of getting results, this only led to me receiving a letter back from the Commission of Judicial Conduct, absolving the despot of his crimes." Dr. Javad hired a new lawyer to change the venue for the remand trial, and to bring the case back to the Boston Probate and Family Court. Despot denied this motion, not allowing the retrial to be transferred.

Time passed. By February of 2019, the remand case had a new date for retrial, toward the end of the month. On February 26, standing before Judge Despot on the first day of the retrial, Herman Goring suddenly announced that he was not ready to proceed. "And in response, the despot told both parties to sit together, and to try to reach an agreement to settle the case between each other.

It's not hard to imagine this scene in a movie. Finally, after all the pain and struggles and delays, Dr. Javad found himself in a conference room with Herman Goring for two hours, where − supposedly − they would come to an agreement, according to the judge.

From the beginning, Goring acknowledged Dr. Javad's fierce tenacity, asking bluntly, "Where did you get all your energy from?"

Dr. Javad responded, by stating, "Please don't underestimate me because of my physical disability. I am much more able than most of you think."

Not surprisingly, this conference room produced no viable solutions or agreements. After the two hours passed, with an endless number of unproductive conversations and negotiations taking place, the two men returned to meet with Judge Despot. Before the judge, Dr. Javad announced that it would be impossible for the two men to reach an agreement that could settle the case between them. "Then, the session ended without any conclusion. The despot stated simply that he was going to notify both parties, in regards to his decision."

A few weeks later, while both parties awaited a judgment from Judge Despot, a discovery master was assigned, by the name of Delilah. Her duty was to collect and report all disputed and undisputed documents, and discoveries, to the court, for the final remand retrial in May, 2019. "After she collected her contractual fees from me and Aya Yakuza, she provided an interim report to the Norfolk Probate and Family Court. Sadly, she turned out to be another procrastinator for the remand for retrial case. Even though she was given an ample amount of time for discoveries from each party, unfortunately, she breached her contract, by not producing any of the requested documents for the remand trial, by me, for the final trial date."

More delays. More procrastination. Week after week, month after month, year after year, Dr. Javad had to keep pushing, and continues to push, as the court system seems intent on delaying everything as long as possible, to shut him out. In January of 2020, after all this time, two days of the trial on remand were finally held.

"I asked the remand trial judge about the final report of the discovery master. I wanted details," Dr. Javad says. "And then, with a fake smile on his face, the despot merely stated that the trial had begun."

During these two days of the remand retrial for division of marital assets, Dr. Javad did his utmost best to introduce all the exhibits that the discovery master had failed to produce for the case. From the outset, though, Dr. Javad knew that he was facing an uphill climb, against a man who was barely giving him a chance. "There was a strong determination by the despot not to allow me to introduce any exhibits for the remand retrial. The despot did not even allow a judgment from Boston Housing Court, which was certified by the same court, to the exhibits." After these two days of trial, Dr. Javad went home, and anticipated the judge's final decision – a decision that he had been awaiting, now, for years, after putting in exhausting time and effort just to get the retrial to happen. He waited, day after day.

And now, at the time of this writing, he is still waiting.

Months have passed. The judge has yet to give his final decision. And Dr. Javad, despite everything he has gone through, all of the battles he has fought, and all the systemic prejudices that have held him down from the start of this terrible process, has yet to see the light at the end of the tunnel. All he can do is keep waiting, hope for the best, and be ready for the next fight, whenever the opportunity becomes available.

For now, though, he is putting his story out there, in the hope that the world may listen, and that justice may be served.

7

A DEEPER PROBLEM

"To me, community is more important than anything else."

Dr. Javad Ghoreishi says this, sitting in his Brookline condominium, and reflecting on the experiences he has been through over the past decade. He is a man who deeply values his friendships, and believes that as long as people are willing to fight for what is right and just, then true equity and fairness is a possibility. Due to his multiple sclerosis, the resulting disability he has faced from it, his divorce, and his background as an immigrant in a time wherein the United States faces severe racial polarization and the highlighting of deep-rooted systemic inequalities, Dr. Javad was not given a fair shake. He was routinely put down, oppressed, taken advantage of, and forced to swallow bitter pills that no one should ever experience.

Despite all of this, though, his tenacity is something that cannot, and will not, be underestimated. While the system itself wanted him to step away and accept a lower position from the moment that Aya first filed for divorce, Dr. Javad has continually fought to break free from all of the boundaries that have been imposed on him, over and over again. When the system told him to stay back and accept the situation, he kept coming back at it, never letting the problems go. When corrupt lawyers swindled him out of money, he had them replaced, and now wants to see their professional credentials taken away. When judges and other officials attempted to procrastinate, and to push his case further and further out in the hope that he would simply let it go, he kept pushing. And when lawyers and other important figures tried to slander his reputation, defy the Americans with Disability Act, and act like he was less than a person due to his disability, he fought back – hard.

However, it is important to know and recognize that everything which Dr. Javad has done, and continues to do, is not out of a desire for vengeance. Justice is certainly a factor, but not the deciding one, either. What motivates Dr. Javad, above all else – what gets back to the importance of community, which he values so highly – is that he knows he is not alone. He knows that so many others like him, whether those people are immigrants, disabled persons, or belonging to other marginalized populations, have been further punished for their marginalization by the same court system that so aggressively punished him. That means that, above all else, he wants to make sure that all of the wrongdoing perpetrated upon him does not get swept under the carpet. He wants to have an impact on these people's reputations. He wants to make sure that they can't hurt other people in the way that they hurt him.

As he puts it, the most important thing is for these people to be stripped of the power that he says they have so wantonly abused. "I do not want any of the people who swindled me to have any public positions. Not as lawyers, not as judges. They are racist, opportunist, and they are harming other people as they have harmed me. I want to put a stop to that. That was why I brought the lawsuits against them, and why I am doing this book."

Dr. Javad knows, from firsthand experience, the numerous obstacles in his way. He recalls that day when he sat in the Canton Police Department, told the chief about his goal of seeing justice served to the lawyers and other officials who had swindled and wronged him, and the chief – while empathizing – said that these goals were too optimistic. Dr. Javad, though, refuses to allow these people to go on without seeing at least some degree of consequences for their actions. As the days continue, and no matter what new obstacles step into Dr. Javad's path, he will continue his fight.

That is why he has written his story here. It is his goal, in putting these events to paper, to weed out the most problematic elements of the U.S. legal system, to see bigoted and prejudiced officials revealed for who they are, and to begin building toward a better tomorrow.

Dr. Javad Ghoreishi has been fighting this battle for a long time. And now, as he awaits the next chapter in his life, he will keep fighting.

Appendix: Relevant Legal Documents

COMMONWEALTH OF MASSACHUSETTS
TRIAL COURT
PROBATE AND FAMILY COURT DEPARTMENT

Norfolk County   Docket Number 11D0426

Kayoko Obara ("Mother"), Plaintiff

v.

Javad Ghoreishi ("Father"), Defendant

On Complaint for divorce dated March 2, 2011. Both parties appeared with counsel when the trial was heard on January 15, 18, and 25, 2013. The parties were given until February 15, 2013 for post-trial submissions.

FINDINGS.

1. The parties were married in Watertown, Massachusetts on September 30, 1993 and last lived together in September 2011.

2. Mother filed for divorce in March 2011. Although the date of service on Father was not established, Father was clearly served by April 22, 2011 when he filed his Answer to the complaint for divorce.

3. Their marriage is irretrievably broken without prospect of reconciliation.

4. There is one child of their marriage, a daughter Sepideh Ghoreishi who was born on March 30, 1995 and at time of trial is 17 years old.

5. Mother was born in 1958 and at time of trial is 54 years old.

6. Father was born in 1957 and at time of trial is 55 years old.

7. This was the first marriage for both.

8. Mother now lives with daughter since September 2011 in a condominium, 99 Pond Avenue Unit number 406, in Brookline, Massachusetts. It was purchased in 2005 for $409,000. 99 Pond Avenue Unit 406 is owned in Mother's name alone. There was a mortgage on that property and the principal balance remaining on the mortgage is now $32,077. The current market value is $390,000, leaving an equity value of $357,922. It initially served as rental property.

9. Since she was a child, Mother has maintained a bank account in Japan. She accesses that account while in Japan visiting family. In 2012 she withdrew from that account while in Japan $7,000 to cover in-country travel expenses.

10. On or about September 15, 1993 and two weeks before the parties married, Moth paid from funds she had saved in Japan $166,976 towards the purchase of a $185,000 condominium Unit 510 at 125 Coolidge Avenue in Watertown, Massachusetts. The balance of the purchase funds came from Mother's sister. Father paid nothing towards that purchase. There was no mortgage. Mother and Father thereafter lived in that Watertown condominium for four years.

11. That condominium Unit 510 was sold in August 31, 2005 for $392,000. These fur were used to purchase 99 Pond Avenue, Unit 406 in Brookline, where Mother and daughter now reside. It is a two bedroom with 1.5 baths. Mother pays her condominiu fee, taxes, and utilities which consist of telephone, cable, and electricity. She is also solely responsible for the condominium mortgage.

12. Mother and daughter moved into 99 Pond Avenue Unit 406 in Brookline in September 2011. Mother made improvements, to the condominium's kitchen and both bathrooms, painted the walls, and purchased new kitchen appliances. Mother produced photos (Exhibit 41) demonstrating the significant "before and after" improved appeara in this condominium. The cost of the renovations to Mother was $60,000 including lab materials, appliances and furniture.

13. The parties' daughter Sepideh is in the 11th grade. In the three months before the first day of trial in January 2013, the daughter stayed with Father for two nights. The daughter also spends a few hours from time to time during a weekend with Father.

14. In the 15 months before trial began and after Mother moved out of the marital residence in September 2011 Father has paid as his sole support to Mother her car insurance expense. Father has paid no child support or other form of support.

15. Daughter is entitled to a Social Security disability insurance dependency benefit a result of Father's medical condition but Father has never given her or Mother any of th benefit. It was unclear when the dependency benefit began.

16. Mother was born, and graduated high school, in Japan. Her mother died in 1989. l father and sister live in Japan.

17. Mother attended dental school in Japan. After graduation Mother came to the Uni States on a J1 tourist visa in 1988 to further her dental education. She initially began work as a hostess at a dental clinic.

18. Mother graduated from Tufts University Dental school in Boston in 1992.

19. Mother began practicing dentistry by acquiring a practice from two other dentists November 11, 1992. The purchase pre-dated the parties' marriage.

20. Exhibit 31 copy of the November 11, 1992 purchase agreement establishes that Mother purchased for $19,125 the ongoing dental practice including equipment locate

77 Pond Avenue, Brookline, Massachusetts which she titled in the names of her and Father. Father paid nothing toward the purchase price for the practice. The parties also assumed the existing lease at that address which did not expire until March 31, 1997.

21. The dental practice purchase agreement called for a series of payments spread over time. Curiously, but without testimony or evidence to explain, it appears the signed witness to execution of the purchase agreement was Mohammad Kochak who later features prominently in Father's financial affairs. The evidence establishes that Mother made at least $16,000 of the payments. The sale agreement for the practice listed both Father and Mother as purchasers, upon Father's advice to Mother.

22. To finance the purchase of the dental practice Mother borrowed $13,000 from her sister in Japan for the down payment. The check was made out to Father on his advice that Mother's visa or green card status would be jeopardized if the check were made payable to her. There was a second check from Mother's sister in the amount of $1,000 which followed in January 1993 also for the purpose of financing the purchase of the dental practice.

23. At the time Mother financed the purchase of the dental practice she was residing in an apartment on Riverside Avenue in Somerville, Massachusetts.

24. At the time of the dental practice purchase in 1992, which pre-dated the parties' marriage by 13 months, there was no mention of marriage by the parties and the Court finds that the purchase of the dental practice in 1992 was not in contemplation of marriage.

25. The parties thereafter jointly engaged in an unincorporated dental practice under the name "Brook House Dental Associates".

26. In 1997 Mother, using her funds, bought the real estate in which the practice was located for $218,000 (see later findings). There was no evidence that Father provided any of the funds to purchase the real estate.

27. Mother met Father on her first day in the United States in 1988 upon landing at Logan International Airport in Boston. Father had accompanied a fellow graduate of Mother's Japanese dental school to the airport.

28. In the Summer of 1989 Mother and Father began dating and dated for three years before they were married. Father moved in with Mother nine months after they met. They lived together for four years before they married.

29. When the parties married in 1993, Mother knew Father had a diagnosis of multiple sclerosis. Up to 1993 Father experienced only mild difficulty, with walking.

30. When they began the dental practice in early 1993, Father used a cane to ambulate around the office reception area. Both parties were working at their dental clinic.

31. Father's physical condition began to deteriorate almost immediately after the 199 marriage and he experienced increasing difficulty moving around.

32. From the 1993 marriage date until the parties' daughter was born in March of 199 Mother did not have to provide any physical assistance to Father because he was then able to take care of himself.

33. After their daughter was born Mother perceived that Father's mood had changed. would come back from the dental practice about 6:00 or 7:00 P.M. and kept to himself often staying in front of the television immersed in deep thought. The birth of the daughter was an unexpected event. They had not planned to have a child.

34. Mother cared exclusively for the child after birth, nursing, cooking, washing clotl food shopping and clothes shopping, arranging for babysitters when necessary, prepari meals for Father and occasionally preparing his lunch.

35. During the first six years of their dental practice together (1993 through 1998) Mother worked four days per week. She took three months off work after the birth of their child. Although they practiced together, each had his/her own patients but Father was responsible for the billing.

36. During the first six years after the child was born (1995 through 2000) Father managed all office and business finances and Mother was not involved in any financial decisions. Mother served dental practice patients, took care of the child and the home.

37. When the daughter began school at age six in 2001, Mother did not immediately increase her work schedule. She continued to work four days per week and did the cooking, preparing breakfast and lunch for the daughter, took the child to school, attended school meetings, art events, concerts, sports activities, violin lessons, and any other child related social events. Father attended only a couple of the child's concerts.

38. When their daughter was about four years old, Mother noticed that the child was 1 attentive and thereafter her academic performance did not reflect her diligent homewoi

39. About one year (early 2012) before trial, Mother took the child to Massachusetts General Hospital psychology department for a neuropsychological evaluation. This wa not covered by insurance. Mother paid the entire $3,600 cost. The evaluation resulted i daughter being diagnosed with attention deficit hyperactivity disorder. Mother took the test results to an institute for further investigation and she also searched and found tuto for the daughter. Mother is entitled to receive from Father one-half this amount, $1,80(

40. Mother now employs tutors for the daughter since three months before trial at a co of $350 per week which Mother pays entirely out-of-pocket. Father paid nothing for th tutors.

41. Mother has also entirely paid for the daughter's scholastic aptitude test preparation and special lessons and language skills. Mother also paid for the child to go to a test preparation program which cost $600, also entirely paid for by Mother. Father contributed nothing to all these education related costs. Mother is entitled to receive from Father one-half this amount, or $300.

42. Mother has Commonwealth health insurance for which she pays $724 per month. Mother wants after the divorce judgment to cover the child under her own health insurance policy because she believes she can afford it and she is uncomfortable with the child being covered under Masshealth by the taxpayers.

43. It was unclear to the Court whether the child is covered under Father's health insurance, Mother's health insurance, or by the State of Massachusetts Masshealth program.

44. Father receives medical insurance coverage under the Commonwealth of Massachusetts Masshealth program as a result of his eligibility for U.S. Social Security disability, a federal program. The daughter appears also covered by Masshealth. This embarrasses Mother who wants to cover the daughter on her private insurance after the divorce.

45. There was no evidence as to the differences in cost or coverage, if any, between Masshealth coverage for daughter and private insurance coverage for daughter through Mother's insurance. Nor was there any evidence as to the cost to Mother for private coverage or the time period for which daughter would continue to be eligible for Masshealth.

46. In Mother's financial statement dated May 4, 2011 Mother listed five bank accounts and total deposits of $127,000. At time of trial these deposits had dwindled to $41,490, none of which are retirement accounts.

47. Father had always been responsible for the preparation of the parties' tax returns for the past 15 years or so and had gone to an accountant tax preparer until 2011 when he prepared his own tax return and filed in the status of "married filing separately".

48. On May 4, 2011 the parties stipulated in a temporary order that Mother would work in the dental practice on Tuesday, Wednesday, Friday, and every other Saturday while Father would work on Mondays, Thursdays, and the alternate Saturday.

49. Mother followed this schedule.

50. Father initially followed the schedule but in the time leading up to the divorce he deviated from the schedule numerous times and came to the office on the days that the parties had designated solely to Mother.

51. Although Father's presence during Mother's designated days did not affect the patients or the dental assistants, Father displayed a lack of respect to Mother in front o the staff.

52. Mother ultimately confronted Father about his coming in on her scheduled days. Mother called security officers in April or May of 2012 on two separate occasions, bot of them on her designated Saturdays, when Father came into and used the office space and the computer. Mother felt uncomfortable, left the dental office and sat on a bench outside. She waited twenty minutes and then called security who went inside and aske Father to leave.

53. In 2011 Mother asked Father to join her in filing a joint income tax return but he refused.

54. In 2011 for the first time since the marriage Mother filed an income tax return in status of "married filing separately", prepared by the preparer that both parties had use over the years, Andrew Schwartz .

55. While reviewing the billing records in preparation of her 2011 tax return, Mother discovered that Father was reporting his patients under her income tax identification number on multiple occasions. She started receiving patient payments from the insurai company for patients that were not hers and reflecting service dates for days that she h not worked in the office.

56. Mother did not claim the daughter as her 2011 income tax dependent because Fat had filed his income tax return first and had claimed the child.

57. Mother's 2011 income tax liability in her "married filing separate" tax status is $24,996. At time of trial she had paid about half that amount and still owed the rest. Oi her separately filed 2011 income tax return, Mother did deduct one half of the commoi office expenses. Mother is entitled to receive from Father one-half this amount, or $12,498.

58. In July of 2011, and pursuant to a stipulated temporary order between the parties, Mother took steps to establish a new payroll accounting system just for herself. Paragr 5 of that temporary order described how the parties will share expenses. Father failed t provide her necessary information.

59. In her dental practice, Mother earns $2,180.75 per week, based on her 2012 annu profit and loss statement which was prepared by her accountant who relied on Mother' "QuickBooks" entries, credit card payments, and her bank accounts.

60. In 2012 Mother twice traveled with the parties' daughter to Japan to visit family. This expense, annualized, is the equivalent of $200 per week.

61. The parties own eight Persian rugs. Three of the rugs are at Mother's residence and have values appraised between $16,500 and $20,500. The other three rugs are at Father's residence and their total appraised values are between $31,500 and $32,500. There are two other Persian rugs which have not been appraised. Mother last saw those two rugs about July 2011 in the living room of the former marital residence in which Father still resides. When she subsequently visited Father's residence the rugs were gone. Father purchased all of the rugs during a trip to Dubai by himself. Mother does not know where he obtained the funds to pay for these rugs. She does not know the purchase prices. The other two unappraised rugs do not appear on Father's trial financial statement.

62. Taking an average of the six appraised rugs of $25,250 the Court finds the value of the other two rugs is $50,500. The Court finds that Father has either sold the rugs or still possesses them. These two unaccounted for rugs are marital property. Mother is entitled to receive from Father one-half the value, $25,250.

63. Starting in about 1998 five years after the parties were married, Father's condition became such that Mother had to help him with certain activities. She helped him put on his shoes and clothes. At that time Father was still able to get in and out of his bed and shower independently.

64. In about 1998 Father began to need a scooter to move about. He had difficulty walking and Mother would have to lift his feet one at a time to assist him to walk. At that point Father was still able to toilet himself.

65. From about 1999 to 2003 Father's condition further deteriorated and his mobility decreased. Father then required even more assistance from Mother, including getting Father on and off his scooter, and in and out of bed and shower. Mother prepared all his meals.

66. From 1998 to 2004, while working full time as a dentist, Mother performed all of these caretaking duties for Father without outside assistance.

67. The first time the parties used aides in the home for Father was Summer 2004.

68. At some point before April 4, 2012 when Father filed a financial statement (Exhibit 7), Father transferred ownership of the former marital home located at 77 Pond Avenue condominium Unit 201 to his younger sister Fatemeh. Fatemeh does not live there. Mother did not become aware of the change in title to that condominium until December 7, 2010 when she received at her new residence a postcard addressed to Fatemeh at the former marital home.

69. During the marriage Father traveled to Dubai at least nine times by himself. Father also traveled to Germany four times, only once accompanied by Mother. Father also traveled twice to Belgium by himself.

70. Until the end of 2010 Father was solely responsible for all the billings, collectior and deposits of funds in the parties' joint dental practice.

71. For a period of five months before a July 2011 Court order, Mother took over the collection responsibility for the dental practice.

72. Mother first came to know Mohammad Kochak-Entezar (hereinafter "Mohamma in 1992, before the parties married. Mohammad then lived in Canada.

73. After the parties married, Mohammad moved in with them for about one year fro August 1992 to August 1993. Mohammad then moved out and began to live in the are Boston University Dental School where Mother attended.

74. Father thereafter visited Mohammad weekly or biweekly.

75. Mohammad left the United States in 2006 for Belgium.

76. Since 2006 Mother has seen Mohammad in the United States about five or six tir

77. Mother has no knowledge of the $24,300 which Father claims to have borrowed from Mohammad between 2008 and 2010 for alleged medical treatment.

78. Mother was unaware Father had any account at the Eastern Bank in 2012. Mohammad's name was added to Father's Eastern Bank account sometime between Ju and July 2012.

79. In about 2007 Father settled a personal injury claim against the Massachusetts Bɛ Transit Authority in the gross amount of $24,000. Mother does not know what Father with the settlement funds. The Court finds that he deposited the net proceeds to a banɬ account (see later findings).

80. In early November 2008 long before the couple separated, Father established a Sovereign Bank account ending in the numbers "5964" (Exhibit 22) solely in his namɛ with an initial deposit of $40,000. Mother up until time of trial did not know of this account and she does not know the origin of the $40,000 funds deposited to it.

81. Father receives monthly disability insurance benefits from Paul Revere Life Insurance company (hereinafter "private" disability payments) for which he had been paying a premium. Until trial, Mother did not know what Father has done with these funds and she does not know when the disability payments started.

82. Father has deposited his private disability payments to his solely owned Sovereiɡ Bank account ending in the numbers "5964". It appears the initial deposits were $5,0 in February 2009, $5,055.80 in March 2009, $4,524 in April 2009, and two separate $4,524 deposits in May 2009.

83. In 2009 the total deposits (all consisting of his private insurance disability benefit) to Father's then solely owned Sovereign Bank account number "5964" were $50,826.80.

84. In 2010 the total monthly private insurance disability deposits to Father's solely owned Sovereign Bank account number "5964" were $61,121.20.

85. In July 2010 Father deposited $17,596.96 into his solely owned Sovereign Bank account number "5964". Mother does not know the origin of the deposited funds. The Court finds these were the net proceeds of Father's settled personal injury claim of which he did not inform Mother. The balance in this account as of July 31, 2010 was $160,216.95.

86. In September 2010 Father deposited to his solely owned Sovereign Bank account number "5964" $30,000 (three separate check deposits of $10,000 each) from an unknown source as well as a $25,000 deposit transferred from Father's Sovereign Bank savings account number "4783". The total deposits were $55,000.

87. In October 2010 from that same Sovereign Bank savings account "4783", Father again made transfer deposits totaling $22,592 (two deposits of $20,000 and $2,592 respectively) to "5964". Father also made deposits of $100,403.24 and $40,000. Excluding the regularly deposited private disability insurance monthly benefit, Father's · total deposits to his solely owned Sovereign Bank account during October 2010 were $162,995.24.

88. In October 2010 from Sovereign Bank, Father made a singular withdrawal of $337,250 and two other transfer withdrawals totaling $18,150 to his Sovereign Bank checking account number "4361".

89. In November 2010 Father made a transfer withdrawal from that same Sovereign Bank savings account "4783" of $4,000 to his Sovereign Bank checking account number "4361".

90. The funds to pay for the family's day-to-day expenses in the 2009 and 2010 time period came solely from the parties joint Bank of America account numbered "6083". Father did not use any of his disability income to support the family.

91. On July 23, 2010, in the form of a bank check payable to himself (Exhibit 39), Father withdrew from Bank of America money market account number "6083" the amount of $90,000 at a time when the account had a total of $231,248.04. On the same date Father had transferred $40,000 to this account from the associated checking account.

92. During 2011 the total monthly private insurance disability deposits to Father's Sovereign Bank account number "5964" were $64,163.

93. In January 2011 Father deposited $90,000 to his solely owned Sovereign Bank account numbered "5964" (Exhibit 22). The source of this deposit was not explained to

the Court nor tied to the $90,000 Bank of America bank check Father wrote to himself July 23, 2010.

94. In January 2011 Father made a transfer withdrawal from Sovereign Bank savings account "4783" of $1,800 to his Sovereign Bank checking account number "4361".

95. In February 2011 Father withdrew from his solely owned Sovereign Bank accoun numbered "5964" the amount of $80,000. Mother does not know what he did with tha $80,000. The Court was also left in the dark.

96. In April 2011 Father made a transfer withdrawal from his solely owned Sovereign Bank account "5964" of $1,000 to his Sovereign Bank checking account number "436

97. In May 2011 Father made a transfer withdrawal from his solely owned Sovereign Bank account "5964" of $5,000 to his Sovereign Bank checking account number "940

98. On some date between May 31 and June 30, 2011 Father changed the ownership (this Sovereign Bank account numbered "5964" from himself to himself and Mohamma Kochak-Entezar. Father did not tell Mother of this change. The balance in Sovereign Bank account "5964" as of the end of May 2011 before the name change was $79,876.

99. As of December 31, 2011 the ending balance in Father's now joint Sovereign Banl account number "5964" with Mohammad was $109,943.92.

100. In January 2012 from the Father-Mohammad joint Sovereign Bank account numb "5964", someone made a withdrawal of $70,000, reducing the balance to $44,838.51.

101. In April 2012 from the Father-Mohammad joint Sovereign Bank account number "5964", someone made a transfer withdrawal of $7,000 to Father's Sovereign bank checking account number "9401".

102. As of December 31, 2012 the ending balance in Father's now joint Sovereign Bar account number "5964" with Mohammad was $37,945.72.

103. In 2005, without Mother's knowledge, Father tried to buy the condominium building which housed the parties' dental practice. He made a deposit of $1,000.

104. The parties have not shared a vacation or social get-togethers in the last five year:

105. Mother took five vacations with daughter: two trips to Japan, February 2009 to Peru during school vacation week for 21 days, to Aruba in 2009 and 2010.

106. During the marriage the parties and daughter took five vacations together, to upst New York, Australia, Germany, Niagara Falls, and San Francisco.

107. When the daughter was born, the parties were living in a one-bedroom apartment. At that time and well before the manifestations of his disability, Father told Wife he was having difficulty sleeping, leaving Mother to solely tend to the infant daughter's needs while Father slept in the living room so he could enjoy uninterrupted sleep through the night.

108. Since daughter was born and until she reached age nine years old, Father has slept in a separate room while Mother and daughter shared a bedroom.

109. Mother is in good health, has no medical conditions and takes no medication.

110. Mother has seen a counselor for individual counseling starting in about February 2011. She continues to see that counselor every week. Those visits are covered by her insurance although there is a $20 per visit co-pay.

111. Mother began marriage counseling for the first time in 2005. Mother and Father attended three sessions together whereupon Father decided to stop going.

112. At a cost of $15,000, Mother had to undergo a dental implant and restorative dental work in December 2010 which was not covered by any insurance. The work is still not complete. She paid the $15,000 from her personal checking account.

113. When Mother vacated the marital home 77 Pond Avenue condominium Unit number 201 in September 2011 she took with her a professional chair, kitchen dinnerware, utensils, cookware, baking pans and a mixer. She had to buy new furniture for her current 99 Pond Avenue condominium Unit 406 residence which she obtained from stores such as IKEA, Crate and Barrel, and a container store. She also took the child's bed. Mother paid $15,000 for the new furnishings.

114. Mother's sole sources of income are her dental practice and a parking space fee of a total of $900 per year.

115. Although there is rental income from the parties' other properties located at 33 Pond Avenue condominium Unit 1008 (titled in the name of "Obara Trust") and 77 Pond Avenue condominium Unit 406 (titled by Father in the name of his sister Fatemeh), the rents have always been collected by Father and he has never accounted to Mother for the rental income nor given her any it.

116. In his May 4, 2011 financial statement Father claimed gross rents of $10,000 from 77 Pond Avenue Unit 406 and a total of $44,308 from 99 Pond Avenue Unit 406 (before Mother and daughter relocated in September 2011) and 33 Pond Avenue Unit 1008. It was unclear to the Court for what time period any of these rents are claimed.

117. Almost one year later, in his financial statement dated April 4, 2012, Father again claimed gross rents of $10,000 from 77 Pond Avenue Unit 406 but no rental income from

33 Pond Avenue Unit 1008 or 99 Pond Avenue Unit 406 (Mother and daughter had moved into 99 Pond Avenue Unit 406 in September 2011).

118. In his trial financial statement dated January 15, 2013, Father claimed gross rent: $19,200 without identifying the location of the rental property which generated these rents.

119. The Court finds that Father continues to collect and keep the rents from 33 Pond Avenue condominium Unit 1008 (titled in the name of "Obara Trust") and 77 Pond Avenue condominium Unit 406 (titled by Father in the name of his sister Fatemeh) at least in the approximate amount of $19,200.

120. Father has paid into the Social Security system for at least ten years. There was neither testimony nor documentary evidence to inform the Court how much, if any, monthly Social Security Old Age benefit Father may be entitled to and when he could begin to collect it.

121. There was neither testimony nor documentary evidence to inform the Court how many years Mother had paid into Social Security. There was neither testimony nor documentary evidence to inform the Court how much, if any, monthly Social Security Old Age benefit Mother may be entitled to and when she could begin to collect it.

122. When the parties moved out of the one-bedroom apartment in Watertown in 199? they bought the former marital residence they still own, 77 Pond Avenue condominiur Unit 201 in Brookline, Massachusetts, a condominium unit and handicap accommodat former marital home where Father continues to reside. The appraised and agreed upon value of the property as of February 1, 2012 is $525,000. Father claims that the down payment came from cash they had as the result of cashing private patient checks. The original purchase price was $218,000 which the parties paid in cash. $50,000 of the ca down payment used to purchase this Unit number 201 came from patient checks and patient co-pay checks for dental services but not from insurance checks although the parties were receiving insurance checks.

123. At about the time the home health aides were hired and to accommodate Father i Summer 2004, the parties made improvements and adaptations to the former marital home located at 77 Pond Avenue Unit 201 at a cost of about $21,000, all paid from joi marital accounts. The bathroom was made accessible to Father so that he could use th toilet and shower. The entrance to the bedroom was enlarged, the toilet was raised, the shower is a "rolling" type from which Father could roll in and out of, and the vanity w moved to under the sink so to ease Father's access. These renovations to accommodate Father, costing a total of about $21,000, were made with marital funds.

124. The original mortgage for jointly owned 77 Pond Avenue Unit 201 was $100,00(That mortgage was paid in full in 2006. There is no outstanding mortgage. Mother believes that the funds to purchase unit 201 came out of a joint account but she has ne' found a withdrawal to match the initial down payment on any bank statement and she

yet to determine the origin of the funds for that purchase. Father decided on the purchase of unit 201 unilaterally and there was no discussion between the parties. Mother did not object thereafter. The property was located by Father. The same blind scenario unfolded with the purchase of 33 Pond Avenue condominium Unit number 1008 which is titled in the name of the Obara Trust.

125. The parties own 77 Pond Avenue in Brookline, Massachusetts, condominium Unit NR1, which houses the parties' dental practice office also formerly known as condo units 102-103. This was two business condo units, since consolidated and now housing the current dental practice, located at 77 Pond Avenue, now known as Unit "NR1". This was a cash purchase in 2005 for $325,000 plus $20,000 for parking spaces. Father claims the cash came from cashed patient checks and personal funds. Father also claims to have contributed cash to this purchase. He claims both he and Mother had separate personal accounts at that time. In 1999 and following renovations these two units were combined into one unit which continues to constitute the parties' joint dental practice location. The cost of the renovations and which funds were used to pay is unknown to Mother. The property comes with two parking spaces. It consists of 1,800 square feet and includes a reception area with five waiting room chairs. The parties share the front desk and reception area. The appraised and agreed upon value of the Unit NR1 property as of February 28, 2012 is $660,000. The dental practice business condominium has no mortgage.

126. The renovation and combination of the two condominium units now constituting the joint dental practice location at 77 Pond Avenue, Unit NR1 required making the patient rooms wider, putting in a handicapped toilet, making the office more accessible to Father, installing cabinets lower so that Father could reach them, making the laboratory bench lower so Father could work with them. Father needs the laboratory bench to access materials for teeth whitening and wax for dental impressions. The entrances within the practice office are also wider. There was insufficient evidence to determine the cost of the renovations to accommodate Father.

127. The construct and function of the dental practice is important to the division of marital assets which includes the practice as well as the real estate. The dental practice condominium "NR1" consists of five examination rooms two of which function as separate offices, one each for Father and Mother. The office remains handicap accessible to accommodate Father.

128. The parties own a rental condominium at 33 Pond Avenue in Brookline, Massachusetts Unit number 1008 which is titled in the name of "Obara Trust" which, as the Court later herein explains, does not exist. Father collects the income from this rental unit and has never accounted for the rental income to Mother. The property was purchased in 2005 for $325,000. The appraised and agreed upon value of the property as of February 1, 2012 is $305,000. There is no mortgage. Father located and arranged purchase of the property without consulting Mother.

129. Mother solely owns 99 Pond Avenue in Brookline, Massachusetts, a condomini
Unit number 406 which is where Mother and daughter reside. This property was
purchased in 2005 for $409,000. Mother and daughter moved into this Unit in Septen
of 2011. The appraised and agreed upon value of the property is $390,000. There is a
mortgage of $32,077, leaving an equity of $357,923.

130. 77 Pond Avenue in Brookline, Massachusetts, condominium Unit 406, was
purchased by Father in October 2010, without Mother's knowledge, for $335,000
(Exhibit 30). Mother was unaware of Father's purchase until she accidentally discove
it in December 2010 through mail addressed to Father's sister Fatemeh. The testimo:
on the ownership was confusing and as far as the Court can tell the property is titled i
the name of Father's sister Fatemeh but Father may have some fractional interest ther
The appraised and agreed upon value of the property as of February 2, 2012 is $390,(
Father claims there is a mortgage on the property, leaving equity of about $130,000. ˉ
Court finds that this was the same month in which Father had withdrawn $337,250 oɪ
marital funds from his Sovereign Bank accounts. The Court finds that marital funds v
used to buy 77 Pond Avenue Unit 406. If it is true that there is only $130,000 of equiɪ
the fate of the rest of the $207,250 withdrawn by Father from Sovereign Bank ($337,
- $130,000) remains known only to Father. The Court finds that Father has or convert
to his sole benefit the $207,250 which constitutes marital property.

131. In his financial statement dated April 4, 2012 (Exhibit 7) Father claimed he has
one- third interest, held by a trust for his benefit, in 77 Pond Avenue Unit 406. The oɪ
interest holder was Father's sister. This Unit 406 was not included on Father's trial
financial statement. Father's testimony on this issue was incomplete and not credible.

132. Mother advertises her dental services in Japanese publications and historically
between 75% to 80% of Mother's patients are Japanese. She has professional colleagɪ
in the area but has not asked them if she could see her patients at their offices.

133. Mother does not want to share the office with Father after the divorce. Mother
testified that Father's behaviors have been such that she cannot share the office space
him. Her trust in him is gone. She cannot conceive of a partnership arrangement shar
with him anything.

134. Mother wants to keep the current dental practice office location. Mother cannot
envision the parties working cooperatively to continue separate dental practices in thɪ
same location because it would be difficult to distinguish and monitor patient records
Further, the Court credits Mother's testimony that Father was disrespectful to her in fɪ
of office staff.

135. Despite a schedule to which both parties stipulated, Father continues to come to
dental office on days which are not designated his.

136. Father changed his office computer password and the staff could not access the billing software for approximately one month. The staff were unable to document their hours worked for pay purposes.

137. Father's staff was using disposable dental materials that Mother and her staff had prepared.

138. For these reasons Mother believes that it is not viable to separate the dental office space into two separate offices at the same location. The Court agrees.

139. The parties share one large x-ray machine which was purchased approximately 15 years ago at a price of $6,000. Each party has his and her own small x-ray machine. The Court credits Mother's testimony that it would cost between $25,000 $32,000 to buy a large x-ray machine now.

140. Mother does not know if Father caters to a specific ethnic or nationality clientele.

141. Mother has been solely responsible to drive the daughter to school and to the daughter's tutor in Lexington. While at the tutor Mother waits until the daughter is finished.

142. The daughter was four years old when Mother first noticed that daughter needed, in Mother's words, "extra attention". Mother brought this issue to Father's attention.

143. Mother did almost all of the caretaking of the daughter, in the beginning after daughter was born by agreement and, after Father's physical limitations became apparent, by default.

144. Mother paid for all of the daughter's evaluation costs. She did not ask Father to contribute nor did she give him a copy of the evaluation report. Father did not offer to contribute, did not inquire of the cost, and did not ask for a copy of the daughter's evaluation.

145. Since the parties' separation Father has not paid any child support to Mother.

146. Father, by his insistence, managed all of the household finances. He did not want Mother involved.

147. Mother never asked Father about the family finances.

148. With respect to the dental practice Father did all of the private (non-insured) billings and collected the payments, did the banking, and oversaw the employees. This was their protocol until the parties separated and Mother converted to different billing software in 2012. Mother however did do some insurance billing for her own patients and Father did insurance billing for his own patients even before the separation. Mother also did some banking but only with respect to her patients.

149. Mother established Bank of America account number "9292" (as shown on her financial statement) after the separation.

150. A Sovereign Bank statement for account number "6249" covering the months of October 2010 through January 2012 (Exhibit 23) establishes that Father was then receiving and depositing therein a monthly U.S. Social Security disability benefit of $1,216 and the daughter's $658 per month Social Security dependency benefit.

151. Mother learned only on the first day of trial that daughter had a Social Security dependency benefit and that it was being deposited to this Sovereign Bank account "6249" which is titled in Father's name in trust for daughter.

152. Although Mother was aware that Father had established an account at Sovereig Bank number "6249" in trust for their daughter, Mother did not know of any deposit withdrawals to that account until time of trial.

153. Beginning in February 2009 the amount of Father's monthly Social Security disability was $1,255 which continued to be electronically deposited to this Sovereig Bank account "6249" from the United States Treasury. Neither Mother nor daughter seen, used, or benefited from these deposits.

154. In January 2012 Father withdrew from this Sovereign Bank account "6249", without Mother's knowledge, $65,000 for purposes unknown. Father has never expla this withdrawal nor reflected it in any financial statements he filed with the Court bel trial.

155. The Court finds the amount of daughter's dependency benefit after September 2 when daughter and Mother separated from Father to time of trial, during which Fathe paid no child support, is at least $11,186.

156. The Court finds the amount of daughter's dependency benefit before September 2011 and beginning October 2010 was about $7,238.

157. Mother first learned of the existence of Father's Eastern Bank account (Exhibit during Father's December 2012 deposition.

158. Father has a sole account at Eastern Bank which was opened on January 13, 20 Father therein deposited $20,000 on January 13, 2012, $6,612 on February 3, 2012., of February 7, 2012, less than one month after opening the account, the balance there had grown to $141,875.65. Between February 8 and March 7, 2012 Father made two deposits, one being his $4,872 disability insurance benefit and the other $4,250 from unknown source.

159. The Court credits Mother's testimony that the cashed patient checks were the so of the funds Father used to buy 77 Pond Avenue, Brookline, Massachusetts

condominium Unit number 406 which the Court finds to be marital property despite Father titling this property in his sister's name. The amount of the patient checks paid to Mother during that seven years period exceeded $100,000.

160. Mother saw cash in bags upon which Father had written "100K". Father kept these bags in a locked case in the dental office to which Mother did not have the combination. In 2008 or 2009 Father opened this case in daughter's presence and daughter reported to Mother that there was cash inside.

161. Mother had observed in the bathroom of the marital home bags on which were handwritten "100K". She recognized the handwriting to be Father's. She had previously seen an unknown amount of cash, inside plastic folders, in the bags. Father at some point had also kept these or similar bags in a briefcase under the counter of the front desk in the parties' dental office. Mother never counted, deposited or withdrew any money from the briefcase. Mother noticed that the money was no longer there in about October of 2010.

162. In 2010 after Father unilaterally purchased 77 Pond Avenue condominium unit 406 in Brookline and titled it in his sister's name, he rented it out at a cost of $2,100 per month until some date in 2011. He has never accounted to Mother for the rental payments. The amount of rents he collected was not established and Father did not disclose these on his 2011 income tax return.

163. On her 2012 income tax return and relying on her accountant's advice, Mother claimed an $8,500 condominium fee and $5,180 real estate tax (for the parties' condominium housing the dental practice) although she did not actually pay these amounts. She also paid to one of the dental practice staff $1,800 for janitorial services.

164. On her 2011 income tax return which she filed in the status of "married filing separately" Mother claimed $11,433 of depreciation deduction.

165. Mother claimed $222.80 per week expense (on her Exhibit 3 trial financial statement) for daughter's tutors, lessons, and sports, is a fluid amount which may change every two weeks or so.

166. Into the parties' joint Bank of America account ending in the number "6083", both parties regularly deposited funds. The account was established before the parties married. Mother stopped using this account in February 2011.

167. The parties used their joint Bank of America account number "6083" for both personal and business related expenses. .

168. In about January 2011 and based on her testimony, Mother transferred from this joint family Bank of America account "6083" to her solely owned Bank of America account numbered "0154" an amount between $101,000 and $120,000. Although the documentary evidence on this issue was confusing., Nevertheless, the pages of the statements for "6083" showing the ending balances on January 5, 2011 and February 2,

2011 demonstrate a total accounts balance reduction from $205,214.76 to $83,617.06 that time frame, consistent with Mother's testimony about the approximate transfer amount.

169. Mothers Bank of America account '0154" at time of trial had a balance of $22,3? (Exhibit 3 Mother's trial financial statement). She spent the rest of the $101,000 or $120,000 transferred funds on lawyer fees, daughter's education including tutors, renovations at and living expenses for her new residence with daughter at 99 Pond Avenue Unit 406. .

170. Father concedes that the marriage is irretrievably broken.

171. Father was born in Iran in 1957 and is 55 years old. He came to the United State 1986 and is a US citizen.

172. Father attended dental school for six years at Tehran University in Iran. He practiced dentistry for two years in Iran.

173. When Father first came to the United States in 1986, he lived in Brooklyn, New York and did research at the Forsyth Dental Center which is now Forsyth Institute. He also did preventive dentistry and microbiology, originally as a volunteer.

174. Father started paid employment at the Forsyth Institute in July 1986 where he w paid $1,200 per month. He stayed there for six years. He then practiced dentistry in Worcester, Massachusetts, working for another dentist.

175. Father has known Mohammad Kochak (a/k/a Mohammad Kochak-Entezar and herein sometimes "Mohammad") for 35 years. They first met at Tehran University der school.

176. Mohammad lived with Father and Mother at some points in 1992 and 1993. Mohammad was a dentist and currently lives in Belgium. Father contacts Mohammad about two or three times per week on the Internet.

177. Mohammad Kochak last came to the United States in November 2012. Father la saw Mohammad in the United States in June 2012. Father spends time with Mohamm: one or two times each year.

178. Father was diagnosed with multiple sclerosis in 1991 when he was 34 years old. began using crutches approximately ten years after the diagnosis.

179. Father began to use a scooter in about 1999. He now uses a wheelchair.

180. Before the parties married, Father took Mother to a multiple sclerosis center whe she learned of the effects of multiple sclerosis. Father did not try to discourage Mothe from marrying him.

181. Father's daily routine is as follows: he transfers himself from bed to the scooter; he waits for an aide for toileting and putting him in the shower. He washes himself, then needs help getting back onto the scooter. He then shaves, exercises and gets dressed.

182. The Court credits Father's testimony that the multiple sclerosis does not affect him very much in his upper body but the effect is in his legs. There is no effect on his mental acuity.

183. Father takes medications to relax his muscles. He also takes an injection to delay the effects of the multiple sclerosis. By Father's own admission, there is nothing about his present condition that prevents him from continuing to practice dentistry.

184.. Starting at some point beginning between 1994 and 1997, for a period of about seven years and at Father's request, Mother cashed all checks payable to the dental practice from patients and gave the cash to Father. The couple had established and maintained a protocol that they cashed checks paid by patients who were not insured. They cashed the checks to avoid paying taxes. Father informed the Court that it was a cultural practice in Iran to pay cash for purchases and not to borrow money. This was not further explained.

185. Father had a heart attack at the end of February 2008. Other than this statement there was no evidence of the aftermath effect on Father or its potential limits on his ability to work in the future. He testified that after the heart attack he wanted to reduce the number of days he worked and his workload. Before the heart attack Father claims to have been working six days per week.

186. Father now claims to be down to two days per week and three days per week every other week. The available billing records do not support Father's claims. What billing records that were introduced established that in 2012 the parties served about the same number of patients.

187. Contradicting his testimony about reduced work after his heart attack, billing records demonstrate that in 2012 Father had 218 patient visits. He was out of the office for about two months. He has a list of 200 patients and he sees about 15 patients per week.

188. Father claims that Mother worked 3 1/2 days per week before and after the heart attack.

189. Father claims Mother now works three days per week. This was pursuant to their agreement to work on separate schedules.

190. After the divorce filing by Mother in 2011, servicing the patients of the dental practice was not difficult but separating the parties' billings and getting paid from the

insurance company was extremely difficult. Mother did not receive payments despite insurance company mailing payments to her.

191. Father was billing for his own patients. He used software called "Easy Dental". Each party had a different provider number. In 2011 Mother's provider number was "0001". In about November of 2011 Mother switched to billing number "0003" and "0005". Father had always used the billing code number "0002".

192. In 2012, both parties used a billing software "Easy Dental" (Exhibit 34) which demonstrates that in 2012 and using his provider number "0002" Father saw 218 pat and billed a total of $115,773.

193. In 2012, and using provider numbers "0001" and "0003" bills were submitted (Exhibit 35) and attributed to Mother's tax identification number for 337 patients. Mother disputes she saw that many patients.

194. In August 2012 Mother changed her billing software from "Easy Dental" to "Dentrix". The software and accompanying hardware upgrade cost Mother $30,000.

195. The effect of Mother's new billing software implementation is that since August 2012 Mother's and Father's billing data are completely separated. From this date, Fat did not have access to, nor could he control, Mother's billings.

196. Before Mother implemented the software change in August 2012 each party had access to the same software and billing records and could have adjusted the other par billing data including the number of patients billed. The Court finds that Father surreptitiously did so in an unknown amount and for an unknown period of years, to : income to Mother.

197. In 2011 and using Mother's tax identification number Father submitted insuranc claims for payments for more than 50 patients that he had served.

198. In 2011 Father also received insurance payments for patients that Mother had se but the number of patients and the total payments therefore could not be determined t the evidence.

199. Exhibit 34 is an analysis of the parties' dental practice billing records, by dentis "provider number" for January 1 through December 31, 2012. Provider Dentist 0002 (Father) saw 218 patients and had total 2012 billings of $115,773 with $99,875 of the amount being billed to insurance.

200. For January 1 through July 31, 2012, billings under provider "0001" (Mother) showed Mother serving a total of only 5 patients and billing a total of $6,899 of whic $1,171 was billed to insurance.

201. But in comparing the time periods January 1 - July 31, 2012 to August 1 - December 31, 2012, a different picture emerges. For the time period August 1- December 31, 2012 (after Mother changed the joint billing software to her own independent billing software), Mother's credited billings, during which she served 154 patients under provider numbers "0003 – 0005", were a total of $156,041 of which $121,146 was billed to insurance.

202. Father manipulated the billing software after Mother filed for divorce to make it appear that Father was earning the majority of the family income.

203. Father admits he has traveled to Germany several times, the last being in 2010. During the 2010 visit and also during a 2009 visit to Germany Father claims to have received stem cell treatment. He did not provide any information about cost, if any.

204. Father admits he has traveled to Dubai more than nine times for both business and pleasure and he normally stays there at least 10 days. The maximum length of his stay in Dubai was 12 days.

205. While in Dubai Father practiced dentistry in the office of another dentist. Father treated patients there and did implant dentistry, working eight to nine hours per day. He saw between 40 to 50 patients each trip to Dubai. Father was paid in cash in the currency of the United Arab Emirates which Father converted to United States dollars. Father claims that he had no accounts in any banks in Belgium or Dubai.

206. Father earned between $30,000 to $40,000 US for each Dubai visit, a total of between $270,000 to $360,000. Father claims to have traveled to the United States with the cash, although there was no testimony or evidence about any customs disclosures to United States authorities upon re-entry. Father never told Mother about these earnings. Nor did the documentary evidence nor Father's testimony establish what Father did with these funds.

207. Father claims he kept the Dubai earnings in a briefcase at his home as well as in the pockets of his clothing located in a closet at the home. Father claims to have spent some of the Dubai earnings on renovating his residence, in purchasing the unit titled in the name of the Obara Trust (condominium Unit number 1008 located at 33 Pond Avenue in Brookline, Massachusetts), and paying the daughter's private school tuition. He offered no documentary evidence to support these claims.

208. Daughter attended the private Waldorf School in Lexington, Massachusetts, for six years. She had to repeat third grade. The tuition there for the first year was $15,000. It increased in the third year to $16,000 and remained at that level through the sixth grade.

209. Father claims that the parties had an arrangement when they started their dental practice together in 1993 whereby he would manage the business finances for the first year and that Mother would manage it for the second year. Father claims that Mother had difficulty managing the practice in her (second) year and she thereafter asked Father to

exclusively manage the office to permit her to devote her efforts solely at dentistry. The Court does not believe Father's testimony in this regard and finds instead that he insi on exclusively managing the dental practice finances and kept Mother in the dark.

210. Management of the dental practice finances involved paying the suppliers, bills condo fees; talking with insurance companies; coordinating with the staff payroll company, unemployment office, Internal Revenue Service; paying the taxes; and arranging repairs.

211. Father entered into contracts with insurance providers in 1993 and has had cont with insurance providers every year since. Except for Masshealth, Mother did not ha insurance contracts with any insurance companies since they began practicing dentis 1993. Mother formed her own insurance company contracts in about 2009.

212. For insurance billings, Father claims that Mother was a "provider dentist" but tl he was the "billing" dentist. He claims, because of this arrangement, the billings for t parties were credited to only Father's tax identification number. Father claims Mothe first became a billing dentist with her own contracts in 2009.

213. Father admits that he kept cash in plastic envelopes in a suitcase since 1994. He acknowledged that he placed in envelopes the cash from cashing patient checks paid the dental practice. He admits that he sometimes took cash out from the bags. Father claims that the cash he took was used to buy condominium Unit number 201 in 1997 which he currently resides (for which the Court notes that $50,000 was the amount p down) and to purchase the two condominium units located at 77 Pond Avenue which were combined into and now are known as Unit NR1 which currently houses the den practice. There was no clear evidence of the down payment if any for 77Pond Aven Unit NR1. A recorded deed establishes that the purchase price for the current dental practice location Unit NR1 was $218,500 on March 28, 1997 (Exhibit 27). No matte source, the Court finds that Unit NR1 is marital property.

214. Father claims, unconvincingly in light of Mother's observations and his own testimony about his cash earned practicing dentistry in Dubai, that after 1997 only a hundred dollars cash was kept in the envelopes.

215. For 2011 Father filed his federal income tax return in "married filing separatel status. Mother asked him to file a joint return but he declined. Father did not ask Mot what her tax liability might be if she filed a separate return for 2011. There was no evidence to establish what tax savings, if any, would have been realized if a joint tax return had been filed for 2011.

216. The Court does not credit Father's claims that he paid 100% of the office condo real estate tax, janitorial service, office utilities, office repairs and phone bills for 201 and 2012 from his Bank of America personal checking account. Although pages from Father's Bank of America checking account ending in number "4822" were accepted evidence, there was no testimony or other evidence to inform the Court which entries

corresponding to checks written were for dental practice expenses. Furthermore the statements titled solely in Father's name began February 15, 2011 and ended May 10, 2011 when the account title changed to Father and Mother starting with the statement dated May 11, 2011.

217. Father claims that the Obara Trust was established in 2005 as a means to own condominium Unit number 1008 located at 33 Pond Avenue in Brookline, Massachusetts. The original trustees of the Obara Trust were Mother, Father, his sister Akram Moller and her husband James Moller. The purpose in establishing this trust was to pay the daughter's college expenses. Both parties agree that daughter is and always has been the sole intended beneficiary of the property. The "Obara Trust" trust document was not produced in evidence. Notwithstanding the "Obara Trust" nomenclature, the Court finds that the parties are original owners, trustees or sole beneficial interest holders and that Unit 1008 is marital property.

218. Exhibit 45A is a deed, recorded in the Norfolk County Registry of Deeds on April 29, 2005, which demonstrates that the parties purchased 33 Pond Avenue, condominium Unit number 1008, Brookline, Massachusetts on April 14, 2005 with title in the parties names as "Trustees of Javad Ghoreishi Realty Trust" dated April 27, 2005. The Court questions the validity of a deed purporting to convey on April 14 to an entity which did not then have legal existence.

219. Exhibit 45B is a copy of the "Javad Ghoreishi Realty Trust" with an execution date of April 27, 2005. This Trust instrument was recorded in the Norfolk County Registry of Deeds on April 29, 2005. The named initial trustees are the parties. It purports to be a nominee trust. Pursuant to direction in the Trust instrument, both trustees must act together to carry out the Trust provisions. The Trust refers to a Schedule of Beneficiaries which is not attached. The Court wonders about the vitality of the title to Unit 1008 given that the deed was executed at a time when the grantee Jovad Ghoreishi Realty Trust did not then exist as a legally cognizable entity.

220. Exhibit 45C is an unsigned copy of a purported Schedule of Beneficiaries of the "Javad Ghoreishi Realty Trust". The beneficiary is "The Javad Ghoreishi Trust Agreement dated April 27, 2005", the parties as trustees thereof, dated April 27, 2005. This document appears not to have been recorded.

221. Exhibit 45D is an unsigned copy of "The Javad Ghoreishi Trust Agreement", wherein the parties are named as both donors and initial trustees, dated April 27, 2005. This Trust is revocable by both of the parties. The parties are the lifetime beneficiaries and their daughter is the remainder beneficiary. This document appears not to have been recorded.

222. In Exhibit number seven, Father's financial statement dated April 4, 2012, he listed his sister Fatemeh as trustee of a trust which owned a one third interest for the benefit of Father in 77 Pond Ave. unit number 406. The value of Father's one third interest

according to Father is $130,000. However Father did not list this real estate as an asse his trial financial statement.

223. Exhibit 38 is a copy of a deed from October of 2010 which establishes that the Father's sister Fatemeh is only an individual grantee of the real property at 77 Pond Avenue Unit 406 and there is no mention of a trust within the deed document. The Cc finds that the funds, $355,000, used to purchase and title this property in sister Fatem name came from Father's Sovereign Bank account number "5964" and these funds constituted marital funds. The equity in the property, all of which the Court finds to b Father's, is $390,000. This real property is thus marital property.

224. Exhibit 22 statements from Father's Sovereign Bank account number "5964" sh that Father's private disability benefits were being directly deposited by the insurance company beginning about December 2008 or early 2009 and ending with a last disabi deposit in January 2012.

225. Father's Sovereign Bank account number "5964", solely in Father's name, was opened in October 2008 with a deposit of $40,000. Thereafter, except for the period December 31, 2008 through January 31, 2009 and December 1 through December 30 2009, deposits other than Father's private disability insurance payments are as follows deposit of $17,596.96 (Father's injury settlement net from MBTA) on July 27, 2010; separate deposits totaling $55,000 during September 2010; five deposits totaling $168,395.24 during October 2010 (three of these deposits, $100,403.24, $40,000, and $5,400 were not transfer deposits; the other two for $20,000 and $2,592 were transfer deposits from savings account numbered "4783".

226. From Father's Sovereign Bank account number "5964" in October 2010 there w two withdrawals ($17,750 and $337,250) totaling $355,000; prior to this flurry of acti the beginning balance for October 1, 2010 was $224,782.59. The $355,000 was used purchase the 77 Pond Avenue Unit 406 titled in the name of Father's sister Fatemeh. T Court finds this to be additional evidence that 77 Pond Avenue Unit 406 to be marital property.

227. Into Father's Sovereign Bank account number "5964", in January 2011 Father made a $90,000 deposit.

228. In February 2011 from his Sovereign Bank account number "5964"Father withd $80,000.

229. In May 2011 Father transferred $5,000 from his Sovereign Bank this account "5964" to account "9401".

230. During the month of June 2011, two months after Mother filed for divorce, the Sovereign Bank "5964" account title was changed from Father solely to Father and Mohammad Kochak-Entezar. The beginning balance then was $79,876.75. Beginning

about February 2012 Father's private disability benefit continued thereafter to be deposited to account "5964", varying in amounts from $5,050 and $4,134.

231. On January 13, 2012 there was a withdrawal of $70,000 from Father's Sovereign Bank "5964". Before withdrawal the account balance was $109,943.92. Father claims not to know about this withdrawal and suggests that Mohammad might have made that withdrawal. The Court finds difficult to believe that a withdrawal of this amount could have gone unnoticed and unquestioned by Father. The Court finds that Father made or caused the withdrawal, for purposes unknown, of $70,000 of marital assets.

232. Father's monthly disability benefit deposit to "5964" stopped with last deposit being the month of January 2012.

233. As of December 30, 2012 Father's Sovereign bank account "5964" had a balance of $37,936.39.

234. Both parties stipulated that 33 Pond Avenue condominium Unit number 1008 is being held for the purpose of paying the daughter's college expenses.

235. Since the daughter will be 18 years old shortly after trial neither party saw the need to seek custody provisions in the Court's judgment. Both parties agree that Father will see the daughter and that daughter should determine the frequency and duration of their contact.

236. Father's claims he established a checking and a money market account at Eastern Bank in April 2012 and deposited to it funds withdrawn from Sovereign Bank because he had a falling out with Sovereign Bank after that bank was taken over by Santander Bank. He was not satisfied with the service, had a disagreement with an assistant manager and a teller and decided to take his business to Eastern Bank instead. He claims all of the funds in the Eastern Bank belonged to him only and that he is holding those funds for his daughter.

237. Father has a sole account at Sovereign Bank ending in number "9401". The Court does not credit Father's testimony that all of the funds herein belong to his friend Mohammad Kochak-Entezar. The Court finds these funds to be marital property.

238. The Court does not credit Father's testimony that since 2005 to time of trial he has been collecting rent on a condominium located at 44 Washington St. in Brookline, Massachusetts owned by his friend Mohammad.

239. There was no documentary evidence to support Mohammad's ownership of any condominium.

240. The only documentary evidence produced at trial about Father's Sovereign Bank account number "9401" showed that it was opened on January 26, 2011 (before the couple separated in September 2011) in Father's name alone with an initial deposit of

$4,256.84. That account remained solely in Father's name through December 2012 despite that Father had added Mohammad's name to Sovereign Bank account numbe "5964" in June 2011 at the same (Sovereign) bank.

241. Upon reviewing the deposits in and withdrawals from Father's Sovereign Banl account number "9401", the Court notes no regular deposit activity of any predictabl amount approximating the rental fee which Father claimed to have been collecting. 1 charges on the account are more telling of the account's purpose: charges were regul; made for what appear to be personal consumption as well as dental practice expense: such as charges for the Registry of Motor Vehicles, Bed Bath and Beyond, Panera B₁ gasoline, Stop and Shop, NStar, Auto Zone, payroll services, condominium fees, Onl television, salon, CVS, attorney fees to Attorney Robert Dilibero whose name appea father's financial statements filed with the Court, Bloomingdales, Sears Roebuck.

242. This documented use of Father's Sovereign Bank account number "9401" cann reconciled with Father's testimony he was simply a conduit for Mohammad's rents. Father's testimony on this issue is implausible and the Court finds these funds derive from Father and are part of the marital estate.

243. Father made similar claims about collecting rent for condominium Unit numbe located at 77 Pond Avenue (in the name of Fatemeh) which, if his testimony were to believed, he began to collect in about May or June of 2011 and continued to time of

244. Father testified the original rent at the Fatemeh-titled 77 Pond Avenue unit nun 406 was $2,500 per month for the first year (2010) , increasing to $2,550 per month June of 2012. Father claims to have been depositing these rents, in the form of check payable to Mohammad, in the Sovereign Bank. Father did not offer into evidence a single check representing these alleged rents payable to Mohammad or which he acc on behalf of Mohammad to support his testimony.

245. Father admits that he did not discuss with Mother using Sovereign Bank funds assist his sister in buying a condominium.

246. The Court does not credit Father's claims that only $30,000 of the funds in the Eastern Bank checking account belongs to him. The Court finds that all account dep₀ in Eastern Bank are marital funds.

247. The Court does not credit Father's claims that the funds in the money market account at Eastern Bank do not belong to him. The Court finds that all money marke deposits in Eastern Bank are marital funds.

248. The Court does not credit Father's claims that within the past five years Mohan has also given him money to deposit into the Sovereign Bank account and it is these funds he ultimately transferred to the Eastern Bank.

249. The Court does not credit Father's claims that Mohammad comes to the United States about two times per year and gives him cash and checks to deposit. There was no plausible explanation offered why Mohammad did not or was not capable of doing his own banking during his visits to the United States or via the Internet.

250. The Court does not credit Father's claims that his sister Fatemeh gave him $40,000 towards the purchase of 77 Pond Avenue condominium Unit 406.

251. Father testified has no plans to move his dental practice if he cannot use the current office space.

252. Father is daily visited by two personal aides: one in the morning and one in the evening, to help him get out of bed, dress, shower, and prepare his breakfast. These aides are paid by MassHealth.. Father also pays, but he is reimbursed by an agency.

253. Father claimed daughter as an exemption on his 2011 income tax return in which Father reported a dental practice business loss of -$29,365. He prepared the tax return himself.

254. The copy of the Father's 2011 tax return offered into evidence is missing the second (signature) page. Despite the mandatory disclosure rule and requests for production by Mother's counsel, Father did not produce a copy of that page which would have showed his tax still owed, if any.

255. Given the earlier testimony regarding his cash-payments practice of dentistry in Dubai, the unexplained deposits to his various accounts and his historic practice of cashing patient checks rather than depositing them, the Court is not persuaded that Father's claimed 2011 earnings are accurate.

256. Father claims that his 2011 tax return Schedule C amount of $83,166 also included deposits for reimbursements of $14,000 that he paid to his daily home health aides. He claims he paid $50,652 of wages to the assistants and receptionist in his office.

257. Father deducted his defense attorney fees in the amount of $11,178 although his described legal expenses attributable to practicing dentistry were only $3,000.

258. Although he owns rental property, Father failed to produce a copy of his federal tax form Schedule E for his 2011 tax return. The Court notes that there is no rental income shown on line 17 ("Rental real estate") on page 1 of his federal return despite his testimony he was collecting rents.

259. Father's disability payments from Paul Revere began in February of 2009 with the first payment of $5,050. The disability income payments he has received with the Paul Revere insurance company are not income taxable and not included in his tax returns. He has received these payments since 2009. He paid premiums for this disability insurance from 1991 to 2008.

260. Father receives disability income monthly from the Social Security Administra·
currently in the amount of $1,165 per month ($268.83 per week), an annual total of
$13,979.16. This is also not income taxable. Thus his total nontaxable income per m·
is $5,958.

261. According to his April 5, 2012 financial statement Father then had $324,200 of
deposits. On that same financial statement he listed only one debt, a loan to Mohamr
for $18,000 for medical treatment which Father claims he received between 2008 an·
2010.

262. Father was unable to explain (Exhibit 46) Sovereign Bank deposits in Octobe·
2010, which were Internet transfers between Father's Sovereign accounts for which t
is no paper record. Father claims savings account number "4783", from which the
transfers originated, is unknown to him.

263. The account maintained by Father at Sovereign Bank ending in number "6249"
titled in Father's name "in trust for" daughter Sepideh. The funds therein consist of
deposits from two sources: Father's $1,255 monthly benefit from Social Security
disability and a $627 monthly deposit representing the Social Security dependency
benefit for the daughter Sepideh. These deposits to this account began in February of
2009.

264. On January 13, 2012 Father withdrew $65,000 from this "in trust for" account
number "6249" and he deposited this to his Eastern Bank account. Father claims tha
of this money is being held for daughter. The Court finds the Eastern Bank funds to t
marital assets.

265. The rental charge for the 77 Pond Avenue, Brookline, Massachusetts condomin
Unit number 406 which Father titled in the name of his sister Fatima and in which Fa
claims only one-third interest was $2,500 per month at inception of the first tenancy i
November of 2010. Father assumed responsibility to collect these rental payments. H
initially deposited rental payments to Sovereign Bank but testified, incredibly, he dc
not know where these rents are currently being deposited, blaming his uncertainty on
Bank. The evidence did not establish when or if Father ceased collecting these rental
payments nor what he did with them.

266. Father opened two accounts, ending in numbers "4882" and "3202", on Januar·
2012 at Eastern Bank in his name alone. In one, a money market account, he initially
deposited $115,000; into the other, a checking account, he initially deposited $20,00·
The Court finds these total deposits, 135,000, to be marital assets notwithstanding th·
date of opening was subsequent to the parties' separation.

267. Father changed the depository bank for his disability stream of income in about
February 2012 to Eastern Bank account ending in number "4882". Although the East·

Bank records indicate that on April 13, 2012 he transferred $12,000 to account number "3202" by telephone, Father denies having done this.

268. Father changed the ownership of the Eastern Bank accounts at some point before June 2012 from his sole account to joint with his friend Mohammad. Father acknowledges that Mohammad was not in the United States when the account was changed. On June 26, 2012, the amount of $15,000 was transferred by telephone out of this account to parts unknown.

269. Father's trial financial statement dated January 15, 2013 shows a total of only $9,000 in Eastern Bank as his "share". Despite the money trail, Father testified the balance of Eastern Bank funds belongs to his friend Mohammad.

270. Father says he has no bank accounts in either Dubai or Germany. He testified he closed an account in Dubai in about 2007. He denies withdrawing funds from Citizens Bank account and depositing it to a Dubai account.

271. Father admitted he previously wired $10,000 to the account of an unnamed friend in Germany but claims it was a loan which remains unpaid yet he does not show this loan on any of his financial statements.

272. Father denies any recollection of another $20,000 transferred by wire to a Citizens Bank account in Germany as established by Exhibit 47.

273. Contradicting previous testimony, Father claims that by 1998 he had discontinued the practice of cashing patient checks and not depositing cash payments.

274. Father admits that he did not discuss with Mother transferring funds out of the account in which daughter's disability dependency benefits were being deposited.

275. Father admits that two years after the marriage he became solely responsible for managing the family's finances.

276. Father was paying the common office expenses for the dental practice by withdrawing marital funds from Bank of America and Sovereign Bank accounts.

277. Father testified that only $37,936.39 of the funds in Sovereign Bank account ending in number "5964" belong to him. Father's testimony that a $100,000 deposit by check payable to Father contemporaneous with a visit by Mohammad to the United States was Mohammad's money and $40,000 was his sister's money is not credible. Exhibit 24 establishes that Father had this account solely in his name until June 2012. No one produced in evidence a copy of this alleged $100,000 check from Mohammed or a $40,000 check associated with Fatemeh.

278. In her most recently filed income tax return (2011), Mother, filing "married filing separately", did not file a Schedule E to report income or claim or benefit from

deductions for the rental condominium unit 1008 at 33 Pond Avenue. Mother reported $240,529 of gross income with $125,163 of business expenses and $23,353 cost of go sold. Her taxable business income was $92,013.

279. For 2012 and based on "Profit and Loss" statement prepared by her accountant, Mother had after-expense business income of $113,398.

280. Filing a joint income tax return for 2010, the parties reported $314,361 of gross business income, $266,799 of total expenses, and taxable business income of $32,493

281. Filing a joint income tax return for 2009, the parties reported $268,358 of gross business income, $209,609 of total expenses, and taxable business income of $48,614

282. Filing a joint income tax return for 2008, the parties reported $312,160 of gross business income, $267,126 of total expenses, and taxable business income of $21,214

283. Filing a joint income tax return for 2007, the parties reported $310,296 of gross business income, $284,858 of total expenses, and taxable business income of $3,014.

284. Given the missing signature page and missing Schedule E from his 2011 income return, given his admission to cashing patient checks in order to avoid declaring taxab income, given the Dubai dental practice income not previously known to Mother, and given his other dubious testimony regarding bank deposits and withdrawals, the Court does not credit Father's trial financial statement wherein Father indicates his gross we business income from the dental practice to be minus (-) $564.71.

285. Based on his and Mother's testimony of the number of hours worked and patien seen which the Court finds to be about equal, Mother's credibly reported 2012 busines income and expenses, the 2010 joint tax return reported gross income, and the 2012 billing records, the Court finds Father's imputed post- expenses weekly business inco approximates $113,398. The Court did not include the Dubai dentistry cash because it was not established when Father was last in Dubai.

286. Father's probable net rental income is $19,200.

287. Counting his private disability income ($4,793 per month or $1,106 per week), I Social Security disability income ($1,165 per month or $269 per week), his imputed approximate business income ($113,398 annualized or $2,180 per week), his probabl net rental income ($19,200 annualized or $369 per week), Father's total gross income a weekly basis, for the purposes of child support is $3,924 (of which $1,375 or 35% i not income taxable.

288. The combined incomes of the spouses exceed $250,000.

289. Father's weekly personal living expenses, as detailed on his trial financial statem are $1,308. The Court finds these states expenses are not unreasonable.

290. The Court does not credit Father's testimony that he owes Mohammad Kochak $24,300 for loans for medical treatment between 2008 to 2010. There is no documentation to support his testimony. This is his only stated liability.

291. Although Father lists on his financial statement $178,789 in bank deposits, the Court must attribute additional funds once possessed by Father whose disposition remains unknown after trial. That amount, of $240,000 representing funds which Father once possessed and whose use or destination could not be established, is calculated as follows: $90,000 on July 2010; $80,000 on February 2011; $70,000 on January 2012. Accounting for the approximate $110,000 Mother withdrew, the difference in the withdrawn amounts is $130,000 of which Mother is entitled to one-half ($65,000).

292. Father has a retirement account in the amount of $56,000.

293. Mother has no retirement accounts.

294. Each party has an automobile.

295. Mother's weekly personal living expenses, as detailed on her trial financial statement, are $1,697.20. The Court finds these states expenses are not unreasonable.

296. Mother's gross weekly business income, as detailed on her trial financial statement, is $2,180.75. based on her earnings during the year 2012.

297. Mother has savings accounts totaling $41,490.

298. Neither party produced any evidence about the value, if any, of the dental practice operating at 77 Pond Avenue, either as a combined or separate practices.

299. On October 4, 2000, during the marriage, from a Fleet Bank account ending in numbers "6083" (Exhibit 36) Father transferred the amount of $10,000 to an account in his name in a bank located in Germany. This German bank account was unknown to Mother.

300. On May 25, 2001, during the marriage, from a Citizens Bank savings account ending in number "4481" (Exhibit 37) Father withdrew cash in the amount of $20,273.93. This account was unknown to Mother.

301. Exhibit 38 is a copy of August 31, 2000 bank transaction, in German language, in the amount of $16,489.16. The evidence on this transaction is unclear. No names appear on this transaction record. On September 5, 2000 Father's signature appears on an apparently associated financial transaction document apparently in German language but its significance and amount were not clearly explained to the Court.

302. If either Father or Mother must relocate his or her dental practice, he or she will need to purchase a large x-ray machine at a cost of about $32,000. Mother will also need to furnish her new dental practice office, all during a time when her sole income (save for $900 annually from parking spaces) is her dental practice which would be interrupted for an unknown time period.

303. Neither party offered any evidence to demonstrate the cost to replicate the practice of either party at another location. Father's relocation would require extensive handicap accommodations for himself.

304. Given that Father, in addition to his dental practice income, has two definite and fixed sources of income (Social Security disability and private insurance disability) as well as rental income which should continue unabated if he were to relocate his dental practice. Mother, whose sole income is her dental practice, should be permitted on that additional basis to remain at the current dental practice location.

7/5/13
_____
Date

_____
George F. Phelan, Judge
Probate and Family Court

COMMONWEALTH OF MASSACHUSETTS
THE TRIAL COURT
PROBATE AND FAMILY COURT DEPARTMENT

Norfolk County   Docket No. 11D0426

Kayoko Obara, Plaintiff ("Mother")

v.

Javad Ghoreishi, Defendant ("Father")

JUDGMENT OF DIVORCE NISI

(On the complaint for divorce dated March 2, 2011. The trial was heard on January 15, 18, and 25, 2013. The parties were given until February 15, 2013 for post-trial submissions.)

All persons interested having been notified in accordance with law and after hearing, it is adjudged nisi that a divorce from the bond of matrimony be granted the said **Kayoko Obara, Plaintiff ("Mother")** for the cause of irretrievable breakdown of the marriage pursuant to M.G.L. Chap. 208, Sec. 1-B; and after the expiration of ninety days from the entry of this judgment it shall become and be absolute unless, upon the application of any person within such period , the Court shall otherwise order, and it is further adjudged and ordered that:

1.   The marriage became irretrievably broken on or about December 2010 and that irretrievable breakdown continued uninterruptedly since then and up to date of trial, with no prospect of reconciliation.

2.   Mother shall have sole physical custody and the parties shall share legal custody of the parties' minor child, a daughter Sepideh Ghoreishi who shall reside with Mother. Given Sepideh's age at time of trial (17), parenting time for Father shall be as arranged among the parties and the daughter.

3.   Beginning retroactive to May 2011 and each and every month thereafter Father shall pay to Mother as child support the amount of $ 627 per month, consistent with the amount of Sepideh's Social Security dependency benefit and the amount Mother requested in her proposed judgment. The Court concludes that application of the Child Support Guidelines in this case is not appropriate because it requires imputed and attributed income to Father necessitated by the Court's doubts about his financial information and his testimony provided to the Court. Father shall continue to pay this amount of $627 per month until the earlier of the date of Sepideh's graduation from college with a bachelor's degree or when she reaches age 23 years old. The Court determines the retroactive amount of child support from May 2011 to month of Judgment to be $13,794 (22 months x $627 per month). Father shall pay to Mother the retroactive amount of $13,794 not later than August 30, 2013.

4.   Neither party shall pay alimony to the other as the Court finds each party capable of self-support, earn comparable incomes and are likely to do so for the foreseeable future especially given Father's testimony about the lack of limitations on his ability to practice dentistry notwithstanding his multiple sclerosis and further given Father's two other definite sources of income as well as rental income.

5.   The parties shall equally share the cost of reasonable extracurricular, recreational, sports, day care, pre- or post school care and educational expenses of Sepideh. Each party shall provide to the other within 10 days after incurring such expense the receipt or bill and the other party shall pay his or her equal share to the other party within 10 days after receiving the receipt or bill.

6.   Father shall keep all tangible personal property in his possession. Father shall keep any automobile in his possession and be solely expensive for its costs and indebtedness.

7.   Mother shall keep all of the dental practice related equipment in the current dental practice location, except for one small x-ray machine the choice of which to keep to be Father's. The parties shall equally divide any fungible or disposable dental supplies and medications. Not later than August 1, 2013 Father shall completely vacate and remain away from the dental practice and the real property located at and known as 77 Pond Avenue condominium Unit NR1 (also known as Units 102 and 103), Brookline, Massachusetts. Mother shall be permitted to continue the dental practice at that location using the current name of the practice "Brookhouse Dental" or its equivalent. Any accounts receivable shall be payable to the parties pursuant to their respective billing provider numbers.

8.   Mother shall keep all the tangible personal property in her possession including any automobile and be solely responsible for its costs.

9.   The parties shall each be responsible to provide and pay for his and her own medical insurance coverage. Whether or not Sepideh is covered by MassHealth the parties shall equally be responsible to pay any of her uninsured medical expenses. If and when Sepideh is no longer eligible as a Social Security dependent of Father for MassHealth, then Mother shall be responsible to provide and pay for Sepideh's health insurance but Father shall be responsible to reimburse Mother one-half of Mother's costs for coverage. Mother shall send to Father each month proof of payment of the medical insurance coverage cost for Sepideh (whether Mother provides Sepideh separate coverage or as part of a family plan coverage) and Father shall, within ten days after Mother sends him such proof, pay to Mother one-half of the cost to Mother. The parties shall equally share the cost of any uninsured medical expenses for Sepideh. Each party shall provide to the other within 10 days after incurring such expense for Sepideh the receipt or bill demonstrating the uninsured portion and demand for payment from the service provider and the other party shall pay his or her equal share to the other party within 10 days after receiving same. "Medical expenses" shall include medical, dental and vision expenses.

10.   The parties shall file separate income tax returns for 2012 and each year thereafter. The parties shall equally share any business deductions. Mother shall be entitled to claim Sepideh as income tax exemption for each year as long as Sepideh so qualifies. . The parties shall cooperate in signing and providing to the other the necessary federal or state income tax forms to claim the exemptions.

11.   Mother shall retain and have the following real property and any interests therein, including parking spaces if any, the total equity value being $1,017,923):
    99 Pond Avenue condominium unit 406, Brookline, Massachusetts (value $390,000, mortgage $32,077, equity value $357,923)

77 Pond Avenue condominium unit "NR1", Brookline, Massachusetts (the dental practice) (value $660,000, no mortgage)

12. Father shall retain and have the following real property and any interests therein, the total equity value being $915,000):
77 Pond Avenue condominium unit 201, Brookline, Massachusetts (the former marital residence) (value $525,000, no mortgage)
77 Pond Avenue condominium unit 406, Brookline, Massachusetts (titled in the name of Father's sister Fatemeh) (value $390,000, no mortgage)

13. The Court notes that the difference in real estate values hereinabove divided favors Mother in the amount of $102,923 (52.66 % for Mother compared to 47.34% for Father. The Court finds this equitable given that Mother alone provided all the funds ($185,000) to initially purchase the parties' first real estate in 1993 before they married which was subsequently sold and the proceeds thereafter used to purchase other marital real property. The Court further notes that Mother alone provided all ($19,125) of the funds to purchase the parties' dental practice in 1992 before they married. The Court notes also that Mother did the overwhelming majority of child care and homemaking during the marriage and provided significant personal care to Father to the extent home health aides were not needed until 2004. This division approximates the request made by Mother in her proposed judgment.

14. Mother shall retain her bank funds in the amount of about $41,490.

15. Father shall retain his retirement accounts in the amount of about $56,000.

16. Not later than thirty days after this Judgment, Father shall pay to Mother the amount of $104,848 (one-half the $3,600 Mother paid for Sepideh's neuropsychological testing, plus one-half the $600 Mother paid for Sepideh's college test prep, plus one-half the $50,500 value of the two unaccounted for Persian rugs, plus one-half of Mother's $24,996 2011 income tax liability, plus one-half of the $130,000 net withdrawals unilaterally made by Father from marital funds between July 2010 and January 2012. The Court does not award Father any additional funds for any handicap access renovations he may have to implement or equipment he may have to purchase at a new dental practice location, considering his other certain sources of income including rental income as well as his unexplained withdrawals of $130,000.

17. The parties, either jointly, as tenants in common, trust beneficiaries or as whatever interest holders they may be, shall retain and equally have and own the real property located at 33 Pond Avenue, condominium unit 1008, Brookline, Massachusetts which they shall use, either by sale or by pledging as collateral, for the undergraduate college education expenses of Sepideh. Not later than five years after the date of Sepideh's high school graduation, the real estate, if it has not yet been sold, shall be sold and the parties shall equally share any net proceeds. If the property was sold before or during the course of Sepideh's college attendance, then any remaining sale proceeds and growth thereon shall be distributed equally to the parties within thirty days after the five years date after Sepideh's high school graduation.

18. The parties shall cooperate to prepare and execute any and all documents, deeds, instruments and recordings to effect the division of the marital property as ordered above. The parties shall equally share the costs including attorney and recording fees. Mother may choose legal counsel of her choice to prepare any such documentation. The division of the marital real property shall be accomplished not later than thirty days after

this Judgment.

19. Not later than thirty days after this Judgment, Father shall pay to Mother the amount of $25,000 as her attorney fees.

SO ORDERED AND ADJUDGED.

7/6/13
Date

GEORGE F. PHELAN, JUDGE
NORFOLK PROBATE AND FAMILY COURT

COMMONWEALTH OF MASSACHUSETTS

APPEALS COURT

14-P-1746

KAYOKO OBARA

vs.

JAVAD GHOREISHA.[1]

MEMORANDUM AND ORDER PURSUANT TO RULE 1:28

In this consolidated appeal from a divorce judgment dated July 8, 2013, and a contempt judgment dated December 12, 2013, and a resulting order for fees dated January 29, 2014, entered in the Probate and Family Court, Javad Ghoreisha (husband) challenges aspects of the property division, the child support order, and the award of legal fees to Kayoko Obara (wife) in connection with both the divorce and the contempt actions. We address the husband's arguments in turn.[2]

1. The property division. The husband principally challenges the award of the parties' joint dental practice (including the office condominium and most of the equipment) to

---

[1] While the correct spelling of the husband's name appears to be "Ghoreishi," we have docketed the appeal under the title given to the action in the Probate and Family Court. See Mass.R.A.P. 10(a)(3), as amended, 378 Mass. 937 (1979).

[2] The wife did not file a brief.

114

the wife. The husband, who is wheelchair-bound due to multiple

sclerosis, contends that the wife's receipt of the handicap-

accessible office effectively prevents him from continuing his

employment as a dentist.

"In reviewing a judge's decision under G. L. c. 208, § 34,

we use a two-step analysis." deCastro v. deCastro, 415 Mass.

787, 791-792 (1993), citing Bowring v. Reid, 399 Mass. 265, 267

(1987). "We first determine whether the judge considered all

the § 34 factors, and no others . . . . We then evaluate

whether the conclusions follow from the findings and rulings."

deCastro, supra at 792. "A division of marital property which

is supported by findings as to the required factors will not be

disturbed on appeal unless 'plainly wrong and excessive.'"

Passemato v. Passemato, 427 Mass. 52, 57 (1998), quoting from

Heins v. Ledis, 422 Mass. 477, 481 (1996).

During their long-term marriage, the parties successfully

operated a joint dental practice in an office condominium

located in the same complex as their home. The parties

renovated both the home and the dental office to accommodate the

husband's physical disabilities. These renovations, as found by

the judge, included widening the office entrances and patient

rooms, lowering the cabinets and laboratory benches, installing

a handicapped toilet, and generally "making the office more

accessible" to the husband. The judge credited the husband's

"testimony that the multiple sclerosis does not affect him very
much in his upper body" and that "[t]here is no effect on his
mental acuity." The judge found there to be "nothing about [the
husband's] present condition that prevents him from continuing
to practice dentistry." The judge further found that, in the
year prior to trial, the parties treated approximately the same
number of patients.

At the time of their separation, the parties agreed that
the husband would remain in the handicap-accessible home. They
further agreed to share the dental office pursuant to a schedule
designating specific work days to each party. The husband
sought to preserve that arrangement, while the wife sought sole
ownership of the dental office as she could no longer "envision
the parties working cooperatively . . . in the same location."[3]

The judge concluded that it was "not viable to separate the
dental office space into two separate offices" and awarded the
dental office to the wife. The judge found that the wife
derived the majority of her income from her dental practice,
"which would be interrupted for an unknown time period" if she
were required to relocate. In contrast, the judge found that
the husband "has two definite and fixed sources of income

_____

[3] The judge found the husband "deviated" from the "schedule
numerous times" by working on days "designated solely to [the
wife,]" and "[a]lthough [his] presence . . . did not affect the
patients or the dental assistants, [he] displayed a lack of
respect to [the wife] in front of the staff."

116

(Social Security disability and private insurance disability) as
well as rental income which should continue unabated if he were
to relocate his dental practice." The judge noted that while
"[n]either party offered any evidence to demonstrate the cost"
of relocation, moving the husband's dental practice "would
require extensive handicap accommodations." The judge further
acknowledged that the husband "has no plans to move his dental
practice if he cannot use the current office space."

Notably absent from the judge's findings is any
consideration of the impact of the husband's relocation on his
"employability" and his "opportunity . . . for future
acquisition of capital assets and income," both of which are
mandatory factors under G. L. c. 208, § 34, as amended by St.
2011, c. 124, § 2. Because the judge's findings do not
meaningfully address those two factors, a remand is necessary
"for that reason alone." Charrier v. Charrier, 416 Mass. 105,
111 (1993).

Moreover, it is difficult to perceive how, on this record,
the award of the handicap-accessible office to the able-bodied
wife could be deemed equitable. It is especially perplexing
since the husband was awarded the handicap-accessible home
located in the very same condominium complex as the dental
office. Here, we cannot say that the judge's "reasons for his
conclusions are 'apparent and flow rationally' from his findings

and rulings." Baccanti v. Morton, 434 Mass. 787, 790 (2001),
quoting from Williams v. Massa, 431 Mass. 619, 631 (2000).

Accordingly, we vacate so much of the divorce judgment that
orders division of property and remand the matter for further
proceedings and findings, and if appropriate, redistribution of
the dental practice, permitting revisitation of the distribution
of other assets to the extent necessary to effectuate an
equitable division on remand.

2. The child support order. In the divorce judgment, the
judge ordered the husband to pay child support to the wife in
the amount of $627 per month, retroactive to May, 2011.[4] The
husband contends that it was error to make his child support
obligation retroactive since the wife did not request any child
support until the time of trial.[5]

"We review child support orders . . . to determine if there
has been a judicial abuse of discretion." J.S. v. C.C., 454

---

[4] The $627 amount was consistent with the monthly social security
dependency benefit the husband was receiving on behalf of the
parties' child.
[5] As for the husband's claim that the judge was precluded from
ordering support to continue after the termination of the
child's social security dependency benefit at age nineteen, he
offers no legal authority to support this contention. A judge
may order postminority support "that continues until a child is
emancipated (as defined by the statutory framework), by virtue
of continued dependency on and domicile with a custodial parent.
This is particularly so when it is apparent from the facts of
the case that the parties anticipate that their children will be
attending college and thus likely will not be emancipated when
they reach the age of majority." Tatar v. Schuker, 70 Mass.
App. Ct. 436, 446 (2007) (citations omitted).

Mass. 652, 660 (2009), quoting from Department of Rev. v.

C.M.J., 432 Mass. 69, 75 (2000). Here, where the husband did

not receive notice of the wife's request for child support until

the trial, the judge erred in entering a retroactive order. See

G. L. c. 119A, § 13(a); Smith-Clarke v. Clarke, 44 Mass. App.

Ct. 404, 405-406 (1998). Accordingly, so much of the divorce

judgment that orders the husband to pay retroactive child

support from May, 2011, to the date of trial is vacated.[6]

3. The award of attorney's fees in the divorce judgment.

The husband contends that the judge abused his discretion by

awarding the wife $25,000 in attorney's fees without providing

any explanation for his decision. It is well-settled that

judges have discretion to award attorney's fees in domestic

relations cases. See G. L. c. 208, § 38; Hoegen v. Hoegen, 89

Mass. App. Ct. 6, 12 (2016). In awarding fees to one party, the

judge must consider several factors, including "the

reasonableness of the fees and the other party's ability to

pay." Caccia v. Caccia, 40 Mass. App. Ct. 376, 381 (1996),

citing Kane v. Kane, 13 Mass. App. Ct. 557, 560-561 (1982). In

the present case, the judge provided no explanation for his

---

[6] The husband further asserts that the "purpose" of the child
support order was "to financially decimate" him. This claim
does not rise to the level of appellate argument contemplated by
Mass.R.A.P. 16(a)(4), as amended, 367 Mass. 921 (1975); thus we
do not consider it. See K.A. v. T.R., 86 Mass. App. Ct. 554,
567 (2014).

decision to award fees to the wife. Moreover, the judge did not

conduct an inquiry as to whether the fees sought by the wife

were reasonable. Accordingly, so much of the divorce judgment

that awards attorney's fees is vacated, and the matter is

remanded for further proceedings and findings. See Caccia,

supra; Hoegen, supra.

    4. The award of attorney's fees in connection with the

contempt action. The divorce judgment sets forth specific

deadlines for the husband to vacate the dental practice and to

make certain payments to the wife. Those deadlines were

temporarily stayed by this court pending a ruling on the

husband's motion to stay filed in the Probate and Family Court.

The judge ultimately denied the husband's request for a stay,

and the wife filed a complaint for contempt shortly thereafter.

The parties entered into a stipulation resolving all of the

issues raised in the contempt complaint, while reserving the

wife's motion for legal fees for hearing before the judge. The

judge awarded the wife $9,115 in attorney's fees and costs

related to pursuing her contempt complaint. The husband

contends that the judge abused his discretion in making such an

award.

    Under G. L. c. 215, § 34A, there is "a presumption in favor

of an award of reasonable fees and costs for a successful

plaintiff in a contempt action." Coppinger v. Coppinger, 57

Mass. App. Ct. 709, 714 (2003). However, "the judge should state specifically in the judgment whether or not [he] is adjudging the defendant guilty of contempt for purposes of G. L. c. 215, § 34A." Poras v. Pauling, 70 Mass. App. Ct. 535, 544 (2007). In this case, neither the judgment incorporating the parties' stipulation, nor the subsequent order granting the wife's motion for fees, contained an "express finding" of contempt against the husband. Id. at 541. While certain circumstances may warrant an award of fees despite the lack of a formal contempt finding, see Cooper v. Cooper, 62 Mass. App. Ct. 130, 143-144 (2004), here the judge's order contains no explanation as to the basis for the fee award. Moreover, the order does not contain any indication that the judge considered the reasonableness of the fees. See Olmstead v. Murphy, 21 Mass. App. Ct. 664, 665 (1986) (discussing relevant factors judge should consider when setting fee award). Accordingly, the order dated January 29, 2014, awarding fees to the wife is vacated.[7]

Conclusion. So much of the judgment dated July 8, 2013, that orders division of property is vacated, and that matter is remanded to the Probate and Family Court for further proceedings and findings, and if appropriate, redistribution of the property

---

[7] Given the lack of a contempt finding, we need not reach the husband's argument that there was insufficient evidence to support such a finding.

consistent with this memorandum and order. So much of the
judgment that orders attorney's fee is vacated, and that matter
is remanded for further proceedings and findings consistent with
this memorandum and order. So much of the judgment that orders
the husband to pay child support from May, 2011, to the date of
trial is vacated. In all other respects, the judgment dated
July 8, 2013, is affirmed. The judgment dated December 12,
2013, is affirmed. The order dated January 29, 2014, awarding
the wife attorney's fees is vacated.[8] Because we think that a
fresh look would be appropriate, the case is remanded to a
different Probate and Family Court judge.

So ordered.

By the Court (Cypher,
Trainor & Blake, JJ.[9]),

Clerk

Entered: March 7, 2016.

---

[8] To the extent that we do not address the husband's other
arguments, "they 'have not been overlooked. We find nothing in
them that requires discussion.'" Department of Rev. v. Ryan R.,
62 Mass. App. Ct. 380, 389 (2004), quoting from Commonwealth v.
Domanski, 332 Mass. 66, 78 (1954).
[9] The panelists are listed in order of seniority.

COMMONWEALTH OF MASSACHUSETTS
THE TRIAL COURT
PROBATE AND FAMILY COURT DEPARTMENT

Norfolk Division   Docket No. 11D0426

Kayoko Obara,
Plaintiff

v.

Javad Ghoreishi,
Defendant

JUDGMENT ON REMAND
(On remand from the Appeals Court)
(On Wife's Complaint for Divorce filed 3/23/11)

This matter came before the Court (Cronan, J.) for a trial on the merits on January 8 and 14, 2020. Kayoko Obara (hereinafter referred to as "Wife") was present and represented by Attorney John B. Jenney, Jr. Javad Ghoreishi (hereinafter referred to as "Husband") was present and proceeded *pro se*. One exhibit was entered into evidence and the following four (4) witnesses testified at trial: Attorney Pasquale DeSantis; Husband; Wife; and Attorney Michael J. Traft. In addition to the one exhibit that was entered at trial, the Court also took judicial notice of the file and the parties' most recent financial statements, Wife's financial statement filed on July 30, 2019 and Husband's financial statement filed on January 14, 2020.

After trial, and consideration of the evidence and all reasonable inferences drawn therefrom, the Court hereby enters the following:

1. **Financial Accounts.** Each party shall retain as his or her own asset any financial accounts currently held in his or her own name free from any claim by the other.

2. **Retirement Accounts.** Each party shall retain as his or her own asset any retirement accounts currently held in his or her own name free from any claim by the other.

3. **Husband's Life Insurance Policy.** Husband shall retain the cash value of his life insurance policy free from any claim by Wife.

4. **Automobiles.** Each party shall retain as his or her own asset the automobile currently in his or her possession and shall be solely responsible for, and pay from his or her own funds, all costs and expenses associated with the automobile.

5. **Personal Property**. Each party shall retain the personal property presently in his or her personal custody and/or control.

6. **99 Pond Avenue Unit 406, Brookline, Massachusetts**. Wife shall retain ownership of 99 Pond Avenue Unit 406, Brookline, Massachusetts and shall continue to be responsible for all costs associated with the property.

7. **77 Pond Avenue Unit 201, Brookline, Massachusetts**. Husband shall retain ownership of 77 Pond Avenue Unit 201, Brookline, Massachusetts and shall continue to be responsible for all costs associated with the property.

8. **77 Pond Avenue Unit 406, Brookline, Massachusetts**. Husband shall be awarded 77 Pond Avenue Unit 406, Brookline, Massachusetts and shall be entitled to retain any proceeds he received from its sale.

9. **77 Pond Avenue Units 102/103, Brookline, Massachusetts**.
Husband shall be awarded 77 Pond Avenue Units 102/103. Within eight (8) months of the date of this Judgment, Husband shall pay to Wife $431,038.50 (i.e. the equalization payment less the $25,000 reimbursement to Husband for the attorney's fees payment). Upon receipt of said funds, Wife shall execute a quitclaim deed assigning all of her right, title, and interest in the units to Husband. Thereafter, Husband shall be responsible for all costs associated with the property.

In the event Husband does not pay to Wife $431,038.50 within eight (8) months of the date of this Judgment, Wife shall retain ownership of the property and shall continue to be responsible for all costs associated with the property.

10. **33 Pond Avenue Unit 1008, Brookline, Massachusetts**.
In the event Husband timely makes the payment to Wife as outlined in paragraph 9 above, Wife shall be awarded 33 Pond Avenue Unit 1008. Upon Wife's receipt of the payment outlined in paragraph 9 above, Husband shall execute a quitclaim deed assigning all of his right, title, and interest in the property to Wife. Thereafter, Wife shall be responsible for all costs associated with the property.

In the event Husband does not timely make the payment to Wife as outlined in paragraph 9 above, the parties shall immediately place Unit 1008 on the market for sale. The net proceeds from the sale shall be divided equally except that Wife's 50% share of the net proceeds shall be reduced by $76,461.50, (i.e. $51,461.50 in order to effectuate an equal division of the other properties and reimbursement to Husband for the $25,000 attorney's fees payment). If Wife's share is not sufficient to satisfy the $76,461.50 payment to Husband, she shall pay same to Husband within thirty (30) days of the closing.

11. **Attorney's Fees**. Each party shall be responsible for payment of his or her own attorney's fees.

12. **Prior Judgments**. All terms of prior Judgments not inconsistent herewith shall remain in full force and effect.

Date: _8/12/20_

Paul M. Cronan, Justice
Norfolk Probate and Family Court

COMMONWEALTH OF MASSACHUSETTS
THE TRIAL COURT
PROBATE AND FAMILY COURT DEPARTMENT

Norfolk Division   Docket No. 11D0426

Kayoko Obara,
Plaintiff

v.

Javad Ghoreishi,
Defendant

RELEVANT PROCEDURAL HISTORY, FINDINGS OF FACT, AND RATIONALE AND FURTHER FINDINGS
(On remand from the Appeals Court)
(On Wife's Complaint for Divorce, filed 3/23/11)

This matter came before the Court (Cronan, J.) for a trial on the merits on January 8 and 14, 2020. Kayoko Obara (hereinafter referred to as "Wife") was present and represented by Attorney John B. Jenney, Jr. Javad Ghoreishi (hereinafter referred to as "Husband") was present and proceeded *pro se*. One exhibit was entered into evidence and the following four (4) witnesses testified at trial: Attorney Pasquale DeSantis; Husband; Wife; and Attorney Michael J. Traft. In addition to the one exhibit that was entered at trial, the Court also took judicial notice of the file and the parties' most recent financial statements, Wife's financial statement filed on July 30, 2019 and Husband's financial statement filed on January 14, 2020.

After trial, and consideration of the evidence and all reasonable inferences drawn therefrom, the Court hereby enters the following Relevant Procedural History, Findings of Fact, and Rationale and Further Findings:

RELEVANT PROCEDURAL HISTORY

1. On January 8, 2013, the Court (Phelan, J.) entered a Judgment of Divorce *Nisi* ordering, *inter alia*, that: (1) Wife be awarded the parties' dental practice as part of the equitable division of marital assets; (2) Husband shall pay retroactive child support to Mother from May of 2011 to the date of trial; and (3) Husband shall pay to Wife $25,000 in attorney's fees.

2. On December 12, 2013, the Court (Phelan, J.) entered a Judgment on Wife's Complaint for Contempt dated October 11, 2013, ordering the parties to comply with their Stipulation of the same date. The Stipulation provided the following:
   a. Wife shall deliver the computer located on the front desk of her office. This is the computer that it not connected to any printer and was previously used by the office

126

receptionist. Wife shall leave this computer with the Brookhouse Security desk within seven (7) days.

b. Within seven (7) days, Husband shall provide an accounting from the date of trial to October 31, 2013 of all rents collected and expenses, e.g. condo fee, taxes paid. Any excess funds shall be applied toward the parties' daughter's college expenses.

3. On January 29, 2014, the Court (Phelan, J.) entered the following Order on Wife's Complaint for Contempt filed on October 11, 2013: "[Husband] shall be charged with $9,115 of [Wife's] attorney's fees and costs and shall pay said amount to [Wife] no later than March 3, 2014."

4. On September 2, 2014, Wife filed a Complaint for Contempt alleging that Husband violated the Court's January 8, 2013 Judgment by being in arrears of court-ordered support payments and college education expenses in the amount of $18,276.45, plus such further amounts as may accrue to the date of hearing.

5. On December 5, 2014, Wife filed a Complaint for Contempt alleging that Husband violated the Court's January 8, 2013 Judgment by being in arrears of court-ordered support payments and college education expenses in the amount of $25,152.

6. On December 19, 2014, Husband filed a Counterclaim for Contempt in response to Wife's December 5, 2014 Complaint for Contempt. In his Counterclaim, Husband alleged that Wife violated the Court's July 8, 2013 and December 12, 2013 Judgments by: "failing to send timely reports concerning any expenses for which she seeks reimbursement, failing to send timely proof of payment for any health insurance or uninsured medical expenses for which she seeks reimbursement, failing to use the condominium at 33 Pond Avenue, unit #1008 as a resource for payment of the college expenses of the parties' daughter, and failing to provide quarterly reports to [Husband] concerning the income and expenses incurred for the condominium at 33 Pond Avenue, unit #1008."

7. On February 23, 2015, the Court (Menno, J.) entered the following Partial Judgment on Wife's December 5, 2014 Complaint for Contempt:

   a. Husband is found to be in contempt of this Court's Judgment of July 8, 2013 for neglecting and refusing to pay child support in the amount of $5,643.

   b. Wife shall have thirty (30) days to produce receipts of the extracurricular expenses and provide to counsel for Husband. Husband shall then pay said extracurricular expenses within thirty (30) days of their receipt.

   c. The issue of college expenses is held in abeyance pending the appeal or an agreement to sell the property as awarded by Judge Phelan in the Divorce Judgment to pay for the child's college.

   d. At the present time, Husband is responsible for $1,500 in attorney's fees payable to Wife's counsel on or before April 1, 2015.

   e. This matter shall be marked up for compliance purposes consistent with the terms and dates of this Partial Judgment.

8. On March 7, 2016, the Appeals Court entered the following: "So much of the judgment dated July 8, 2013, that orders division of property is vacated, and that matter is remanded to the Probate and Family Court for further proceedings and findings, and if appropriate, redistribution

127

of the property consistent with this memorandum and order. So much of the judgment that orders attorney's fees is vacated, and that matter is remanded for further proceedings and findings consistent with this memorandum and order. So much of the judgment that orders the husband to pay child support from May, 2011, to the date of trial is vacated. In all other respects, the judgment dated July 8, 2013, is affirmed. The judgment dated December 12, 2013, is affirmed. The order dated January 29, 2014, awarding the wife attorney's fees is vacated."

9. On March 29, 2016, Wife filed a Complaint for Contempt alleging that Husband violated the Court's July 8, 2013 Judgment by: "sitting next to the door and intimidating [Wife] by remaining there and watching all actions on the other side of [the] glass window."

10. On December 20, 2016, the Court (Menno, J.) entered the following Order: "The Court continues this matter due to the present investigation by the Board of Dental Registration into whether or not [Husband] can practice dentistry at this time. There is no definitive date when the investigation shall be concluded. The Court agrees with [Wife's] counsel that this issue is pivotal and at the heart of the remand decision by the Appeals Court. Therefore, this matter is continued generally until the investigation is concluded and a determination is made by the Board. It shall be the obligation of counsel to notify this Court immediately upon the same. At that time, a new trial date and status conference shall be assigned."

11. On May 10, 2017, the Court (Menno, J.) entered an Order after remand which provided, *inter alia*, that:

    a. The Board of Dental Registration has drafted a Consent Agreement between the Board and Husband. Husband has not signed the agreement, but has stated through his counsel in this matter that he will sign it upon this Court entering a specific order. He seeks the Court to enter a specific order allowing him access for an approximate six month period of time to the dental office that is handicap accessible to basically conduct a practice skill session over time and then complete dental procedures on willing patients that will be evaluated by a dental professional.

    b. The Court orders Husband to inquire of the Board of Dental Registration as to what other options for a facility or office in order for him to do his practice skill work and actual procedures that will be evaluated. The Court is referring to either a dental school for example or an office of another dentist. This Court is not convinced at this time that he can only complete this process in the former marital dental office, now occupied by Wife. The Court has reviewed the Consent Agreement and there is no provision relating to the actual facility or place for the evaluation to occur.

    c. After Husband has obtained this information and exhausted all other alternatives and filed an affidavit with this Court through his counsel of same, then this Court will rule on whether or not he can have one day a week access to the present dental office of Wife for the requested approximate six month time to complete this process.

12. On January 12, 2018, Husband filed a Complaint for Contempt alleging that Wife failed to comply with the subpoenas he served her with on December 8, 2017.

13. On January 8, 2019, the Court (Cronan, J.) entered an Order pertaining to discovery which provided, *inter alia*, that:

a. Wife shall provide Husband with copies of her 2015-2017 business tax returns with all schedules within ten (10) days.
b. Wife shall allow access to the dental office to Ed Ferrero of DDS Match Company New England within twenty-one (21) days so the practice may be appraised.
c. Husband shall produce documents responsive to Wife's Request for Production dated 10/9/18 within twenty-one days.

14. On February 19, 2019, Husband filed a Complaint for Contempt alleging that Wife violated the Court's January 8, 2019 Order by failing to provide her business tax returns for 2015-2017 and by failing to allow his appraiser access to the dental practice.

15. On March 7, 2019, Wife filed a Complaint for Contempt alleging that Husband violated the Court's January 8, 2019 Order by failing to respond to Wife's Request for Production of Documents within twenty-one days as ordered by the Court.

16. On March 18, 2019, the Court (Cronan, J.) entered a Temporary Order appointing Jennifer Roman, Esq. as Special Master for Discovery (hereinafter "Discovery Master").

17. On April 22, 2019, Husband filed a Complaint for Contempt seeking reimbursement for the attorney's fees he paid to Wife in the amount of $25,000 as said order was vacated by the Appeals Court.

18. On May 7, 2019, the Discovery Master filed an Interim Discovery Master Report and Order which provided, *inter alia*, that: "I reserve all recommendations and orders regarding the parties' ongoing discovery dispute in this current litigation, as well as which party, if either, acted in bad faith in connection with discovery leading up to the ultimate disposition of this matter."

19. On July 31, 2019, the Discovery Master filed a Second Interim Discovery Master Report and Order which also reserved all recommendations and orders regarding the parties' ongoing discovery dispute.

20. On August 1, 2019, the Court (Cronan, J.) entered an Order consolidating Wife's March 7, 2019 Complaint for Contempt with the trial on remand scheduled for January 8, 2020 and January 14, 2020.

FINDINGS OF FACT

Basic Factual Information

1. The Court hereby incorporates the Court's (Phelan, J.) Findings of Fact entered on July 5, 2013, except as modified or supplemented herein.

2. The parties were married on September 30, 1993 in Watertown, Massachusetts.

3. There was one child born of the marriage, Sepideh Ghoreishi, born on March 30, 1995. In 2019, Sepideh graduated from the University of Massachusetts Boston.

4. The parties last lived together at 77 Pond Avenue Unit 201, Brookline, Massachusetts (hereinafter "the marital home") on or about September of 2011.

5. This is the first marriage for both parties.

6. Wife currently resides at 99 Pond Avenue Unit 406, Brookline, Massachusetts.

7. Husband currently resides at the marital home.

Length of the Marriage

8. The parties were married on September 30, 1993. For purposes of property division, the parties were married for 19.25 years at the time of the Judgment of Divorce.

Age of the Parties

9. Wife was born on July 7, 1958 and was sixty-one years old at the time of trial.

10. Husband was born on December 12, 1957 and was sixty-two years old at the time of trial.

Health of the Parties

11. Wife is in good health.

12. Husband suffers from Multiple Sclerosis (hereinafter "MS").

13. In 1993, Husband began using a cane. Wife assisted Husband at work during this time.

14. In approximately 1997, Husband began to use a motorized scooter. Once Husband began utilizing a motorized scooter, Wife began to help Husband shower and get dressed.

15. In 2004, an aid started to come to the marital home to help Husband. Around 2009, the parties hired a second aid to come into the home.

16. Currently, Husband has a personal assistant who helps him get dressed and to get in and out of bed. Husband also hires someone to come into the home to cook and clean.

17. Husband testified that he has had two "angios", one in 2008 and one in 2019. In the summer of 2019, Husband underwent stent placement surgery.

Station in Life

18. The parties lived an upper-middle-income lifestyle during the marriage, owning their own business, owning several real properties, and sending their daughter to private elementary and middle school.

130

Occupation, Vocational Skills, Employability, and Income

19. In 1983, Wife graduated from Nihon University dental school in Japan. Wife worked as a dentist in Japan until she came to the United States in 1988. When she first arrived in the United States, Wife worked at Forsyth Dental Center in Boston. She then went to dental school in Birmingham, Alabama to further her education. In Alabama, Wife worked as a research fellow for six to eight months. In 1990, Wife returned to Boston to go to Tufts Dental School; she graduated in 1992 and worked as a dental hygienist until December of 1992.

20. In November of 1992, Wife purchased the parties' dental office, Brookhouse Dental Associates, for approximately $16,000. Wife received a loan from her sister to make the purchase which has since been repaid.

21. In January of 1993, Wife became a licensed dentist.

22. At the time of the divorce, Wife had weekly income from her dental practice of $2,180.75.

23. Currently, Wife earns weekly income from the dental practice in the amount of $784. She also receives rental income in the amount of $242 per week from the parties' rental unit located at 33 Pond Avenue Unit 1008, Brookline, Massachusetts.

24. Husband attended dental school at Tehran University in Iran. He practiced dentistry in Iran for two years and then he moved to the United States in 1986.

25. In January of 1993, Husband began working with Wife at Brookhouse Dental Associates.

26. At the time of the divorce, the Court found that Husband had the following weekly income: $1,106 in private disability income, $269 per week in social security disability income, imputed business income of $2,180, and net rental income for Unit 1008 and 77 Pond Avenue Unit 406 in the amount of $369.

27. Currently, Husband receives social security disability and private disability income in the total amount of $1,652 per week. Husband does not currently have any other sources of income.

28. Husband testified that his MS does not prevent him from working in the parties' dental office, which was modified to accommodate his needs. With a trained dental assistant, Husband is able to perform the tasks required to practice dentistry, including using a dental drill. For any procedures Husband cannot perform, he testified that he can bring in another dentist. Until Wife was awarded the dental office in the Judgment of Divorce, Husband taught dentistry at the parties' office through the APEX program at Boston University Graduate School of Dentistry.

29. As described in the procedural history above, the Board of Dental Registration (hereinafter "the Board") commenced an investigation into Husband's ability to practice dentistry in

approximately 2016.[1] No evidence was provided regarding the outcome of the Board's investigation. Husband testified that he did not sign the Consent Agreement provided to him by the Board. The Court is unaware of how, if at all, this affects Husband's ability to practice dentistry.

30. Currently, Husband is performing dental research. He has four United States patents, including for toothpaste, hemorrhoid cream, and a cushion to prevent finger numbness. The toothpaste patent is a provisional patent. Husband's hemorrhoid cream patent is also registered with the World Intellectual Property Organization headquartered in Switzerland. Additionally, Husband formed an S corporation relative to pharmacy, Batool Pharma International, Inc. Husband performs most of his work from home. He does not receive income from his research or business ventures.

Estate of the Parties

31. At the time of the divorce, Wife had bank accounts with a total balance of $41,490.

32. Currently, Wife has two Bank of America checking accounts with a total balance of $46,900. Additionally, Wife has two retirement accounts with a total value of $23,000.

33. Wife owns a 2008 Dodge Caravan with a current fair market value of $3,000.

34. At the time of the divorce, Husband had retirement accounts with a total value of $56,000.

35. Currently, Husband has two checking accounts with a total balance of $58,307. Additionally, Husband has a profit sharing account with a current value of $6,859.76 and a life insurance policy with a cash value of $110,000.

36. Husband owns a 2011 Honda Minivan with a fair market value of $1,500.

37. The only personal property the parties testified to were six Persian rugs. The Court hereby adopts the Court's (Phelan, J.) Findings of Fact dated July 5, 2013 regarding the Persian rugs. Accordingly, the Court does not find it necessary to make any orders for reimbursement to Husband for funds he was ordered to pay to Wife pursuant to paragraph 16 of the Judgment of Divorce.[2]

38. At the time of the divorce, the parties owned five condominiums in the same complex in Brookline, Massachusetts, Brookhouse Condominium: 99 Pond Avenue Unit 406, which is Wife's residence; 77 Pond Avenue Units 102/103, which is the parties' dental office; 77

---

[1] Husband alleges that the Board's investigation was the result of a letter sent to the Board by Attorney Janney. Husband filed a lawsuit against Attorney Janney in Norfolk Superior Court. The case was transferred to Suffolk Superior Court and was ultimately dismissed.

[2] Paragraph 16 of the Judgment of Divorce provides, *inter alia*, the following: "Not later than thirty days after this Judgment, [Husband] shall pay to [Wife] the amount of $104,848 (one-half the $3,600 [Wife] paid for Sepideh's neuropsychological testing, plus one-half the $600 [Wife] paid for Sepideh's college test prep, plus one-half the $50,500 value of two unaccounted for Persian rugs, plus one-half of [Wife's] $24,996 2011 income tax liability, plus one-half of the $130,000 net withdrawals unilaterally made by [Husband] from marital funds between July 2010 and January 2012."

Pond Avenue Unit 201, the marital home, in which Husband resides; 33 Pond Avenue Unit 1008, which is a rental property; and 77 Pond Avenue Unit 406, which Husband sold on October 23, 2018 for approximately $719,000.[3]

39. In the Judgment of Divorce entered on July 8, 2013, Wife was awarded 99 Pond Avenue Unit 406 and 77 Pond Avenue Units 102, 103, which are currently in Wife's name. Husband was awarded 77 Pond Avenue Unit 201 and 77 Pond Avenue Unit 406; Unit 201 is currently in Husband's name. The parties were ordered to maintain the rental property located at 33 Pond Avenue Unit 1008 in order to fund Sepideh's education; the parties currently jointly own this property.

99 Pond Avenue Unit 406

40. In July of 1993, Wife purchased a residential condominium located at 126 Coolidge Avenue Unit 510, Watertown, Massachusetts (hereinafter "the Watertown property"). She utilized funds she inherited from her mother in order to make the purchase. Husband resided with Wife in the Watertown property until the parties purchased the marital home in 1996.

41. In 2005, Wife sold the Watertown property and used the proceeds to purchase 99 Pond Avenue Unit 406, where she currently resides. The purchase price of 99 Pond Avenue Unit 406 was $409,000. The proceeds from the sale of the Watertown property were $360,000 and Wife financed the remainder of the purchase.

42. From 2005 until September of 2011, when Wife moved out of the marital home and into 99 Pond Avenue Unit 406, Wife rented the property and used the rental income to pay for household expenses.

43. At the time of the divorce, the parties stipulated that 99 Pond Avenue Unit 406 had a fair market value of $390,000 and was encumbered by a mortgage in the amount of $32,077, thereby leaving equity of $357,923. Currently, Wife values the property at $645,900. The property is encumbered by a mortgage in the amount of $19,710, thereby leaving equity of $626,190.

77 Pond Avenue Unit 201

44. In 1996, the parties purchased 77 Pond Avenue Unit 201, which was the marital home.

45. At the time of the divorce, the parties stipulated that the marital home had a fair market value of $525,000; there was no mortgage on the property. Husband testified that he believes the current fair market value of the property is $900,000.

---

[3] The Court finds it equitable to adopt the stipulated-to values of the properties at the time of the divorce due to the length of time that has passed between the divorce trial and the remand trial, as well as the lack of credible evidence admitted at the remand trial regarding the properties' current values.

46. In 1997, the parties purchased 77 Pond Avenue Units 102/103 (hereinafter "Units 102/103"), the condominium in which the parties' dental office is located. At the time of the purchase, Unit 102 and Unit 103 were two separate units. The parties' renovated Units 102/103 to form one dental office. The parties renovated Units 102/103 to accommodate Husband's needs.

47. At the time of the divorce, the parties stipulated that Units 102/103 had a fair market value of $660,000; there was no mortgage on the property. Currently, Wife values the property at $985,600 and Husband values the property at $1,035,400.

48. No evidence was presented regarding the value of Brookhouse Dental Associates, only the condominium in which the property is located.

33 Pond Avenue Unit 1008

49. In 2004, the parties purchased 33 Pond Avenue Unit 1008 (hereinafter "Unit 1008") for $248,000 which they utilized as a rental property. During the marriage, Husband was responsible for paying the bills for the property and for collecting the rent.

50. In October of 2013, Wife took over management of the property. She currently receives net weekly rental income of $242.

51. At the time of the divorce, the parties stipulated that Unit 1008 had a fair market of $305,000; there was no mortgage on the property. Currently, Husband values the property at $539,000.

77 Pond Avenue Unit 406

52. In October of 2010, without Wife's knowledge, Husband purchased 77 Pond Avenue Unit 406 for $335,000. That same month, Husband withdrew $337,250 of marital funds. At the time of the divorce, the parties stipulated that the property had a fair market value of $390,000. Husband testified at the divorce trial that the property was encumbered by a mortgage in the amount of $130,000. The Court (Phelan, J.) determined that there was either no mortgage on the property, or Husband converted $207,250 of marital property for his sole benefit. Accordingly, the Court (Phelan, J.) utilized the $390,000 value in its equitable division of marital property.

53. Despite using marital funds to purchase the property, Husband had the property titled in the name of his sister, Fatemeh Ghoreishi (hereinafter "Fatemeh"). At trial, an affidavit of Fatemeh dated August 4, 2018 was entered as an exhibit. In the affidavit, Fatemeh states that she gave title to the property to Husband in exchange for a property Husband inherited in Iran. Fatemeh also states in her affidavit that 77 Pond Avenue Unit 406 has a fair market value of $745,000 and the property in Iran is of equal or greater value.

54. On October 23, 2018, Husband sold 77 Pond Avenue Unit 406 for $719,000. The Court does not credit Husband's testimony that he does not know what happened to the proceeds from the sale, which he estimated to be approximately $600,000.

55. Wife has total weekly deductions from pay of $387 and total weekly expenses not deducted from pay in the amount of $794. Accordingly, Wife's weekly expenses exceed her weekly income by $155, the Court finds that Wife is capable of supporting herself. At the time of the divorce, Wife was receiving weekly income from her dental office in the amount of $2,180.75, $1,396.75 per week more than she is currently earning from the dental office.

56. Husband has total weekly deductions from pay in the amount of $45 and total weekly expenses not deducted from pay in the amount of $1,525. Husband has the ability to meet his weekly expenses.

Liabilities

57. Wife does not have any liabilities.

58. Husband does not have any liabilities.

Opportunity to Acquire Future Assets and Income

59. Wife has the opportunity to acquire future assets and income through her practice of dentistry.

60. Husband has the opportunity to acquire future assets and income through his practice of dentistry and through receipt of social security disability and private disability income.

Conduct/Contribution

61. Wife was the primary caretaker of the parties' daughter. She was also primarily responsible for the household responsibilities, including cooking, cleaning, and laundry.

62. Both parties worked full-time from the start of the marriage until September of 1998. At that time, Wife began working three and a half days per week so she could be more available to care for Sepideh and Husband.

63. Sepideh attended private school from kindergarten through eighth grade. From kindergarten through third grade, Sepideh attended the Lincoln School in Brookline and from third grade through eighth grade, Sepideh attended the Waldorf School. The Waldorf School was thirty minutes away from the marital home and Wife was responsible for transportation. However, Husband occasionally picked Sepideh up from school.

64. Wife helped Sepideh with the college admissions process. For her freshman year of college, Sepideh attended Quinnipiac University as a residential student. She then transferred and commuted to the University of Massachusetts Boston, graduating in 2019. Wife paid for Sepideh's first year of college and the remainder was paid for with the rental income from Unit 1008.

65. During the marriage, Husband was responsible for the parties' finances.

66. From 1993 to 1994, Wife managed the dental office. Thereafter, the parties shared the responsibility of running the office. Wife was responsible for supplies, billing, and interviewing and training employees. Husband was responsible for the payroll and both parties made the hiring decisions.

67. Husband testified extensively regarding an issue with the deeds the parties executed pertaining to their real properties following receipt of the Judgment of Divorce. The Court is unclear regarding exactly what happened as no deeds were admitted into evidence, but apparently there was a clerical error regarding which names were on which deeds. As soon as the error was discovered, the deeds were corrected.[4]

Attorney's Fees

68. On March 7, 2016, the Appeals Court entered the following: "So much of the judgment that orders attorney's fees is vacated, and that matter is remanded for further proceedings and findings consistent with this memorandum and order."

69. Attorney Pasquale DeSantis (hereinafter "Attorney DeSantis") works at the law firm, Prince Lobel which represented Wife in the divorce. Attorney DeSantis testified at trial and submitted to the Court Proposed Findings of Fact and Conclusions of Law in Support of Motion for Award of Attorney's Fees. The Court does not find Attorney DeSantis's testimony or proposal sufficient to justify an award of attorney's fees to Wife on the Complaint for Divorce. Much of the proposal addresses the Court's January 29, 2014 Order for attorney's fees on Wife's Complaint for Contempt, but that award was simply vacated by the Appeals Court, not remanded. Wife provided no further evidence supporting the award of attorney's fees to her in the divorce matter. Accordingly, each party shall be responsible for payment of his or her own attorney's fees.

Complaints for Contempt

70. On September 2, 2014, Wife filed a Complaint for Contempt alleging that Husband violated the Court's January 8, 2013 Judgment by being in arrears of court-ordered support payments and college education expenses in the amount of $18,276.45, plus such further amounts as may accrue to the date of hearing.

71. On December 5, 2014, Wife filed a Complaint for Contempt alleging that Husband violated the Court's January 8, 2013 Judgment by being in arrears of court-ordered support payments and college education expenses in the amount of $25,152.

72. On December 19, 2014, Husband filed a Counterclaim for Contempt in response to Wife's December 5, 2014 Complaint for Contempt. In his Counterclaim, Husband alleged that Wife violated the Court's July 8, 2013 and December 12, 2013 Judgments by: "failing to send

---

[4] Husband alleges that his name was forged on the deeds by Attorney Pasquale DeSantis. During his testimony, Attorney DeSantis adamantly denied the allegation. Husband filed charges against Attorney DeSantis with the Brookline Police Department, the Canton Police Department, and the Attorney General; no charges have been filed against Attorney DeSantis. Also in regard to this allegation, Husband filed a lawsuit against Attorney DeSantis in Norfolk Superior Court and the case was transferred to Suffolk Superior Court. The Court has no further information regarding the status of the Superior Court action.

timely reports concerning any expenses for which she seeks reimbursement, failing to send timely proof of payment for any health insurance or uninsured medical expenses for which she seeks reimbursement, failing to use the condominium at 33 Pond Avenue, unit #1008 as a resource for payment of the college expenses of the parties' daughter, and failing to provide quarterly reports to [Husband] concerning the income and expenses incurred for the condominium at 33 Pond Avenue, unit #1008."

73. On February 23, 2015, the Court (Menno, J.) entered a Partial Judgment on Wife's December 5, 2014 Complaint for Contempt. No evidence was provided regarding whether Husband continues to remain in arrears of court-ordered support payments. Accordingly, the Court shall enter a Further Judgment finding Husband not in contempt except as provided in the February 23, 2015 Partial Judgment. Additionally, Husband provided no evidence regarding the allegations in his December 19, 2014 Counterclaim. Accordingly, the Court shall enter a Judgment finding Wife not in contempt. The Court shall also enter a Judgment on Wife's September 2, 2014 Complaint for Contempt finding Husband not in contempt.

74. On March 29, 2016, Wife filed a Complaint for Contempt alleging that Husband violated the Court's July 8, 2013 Judgment by: "sitting next to the door and intimidating [Wife] by remaining there and watching all actions on the other side of [the] glass window." Wife provided no evidence of this claim. Accordingly, the Court shall enter a Judgment finding Husband not in contempt.

75. On January 12, 2018, Husband filed a Complaint for Contempt alleging that Wife failed to comply with the subpoenas he served her with on December 8, 2017.

76. On February 19, 2019, Husband filed a Complaint for Contempt alleging that Wife violated the Court's January 8, 2019 Order by failing to provide her business tax returns for 2015-2017 and by failing to allow his appraiser access to the dental practice.

77. On March 7, 2019, Wife filed a Complaint for Contempt alleging that Husband violated the Court's January 8, 2019 Order by failing to respond to Wife's Request for Production of Documents within twenty-one days as ordered by the Court.

78. Neither party called the Discovery Master as a witness at trial, nor did either party provide sufficient evidence that the other was is in contempt regarding discovery matters. Accordingly, the Court shall enter separate judgments finding Wife not in contempt on Husband's January 12, 2018 Complaint for Contempt, finding Wife not in contempt on Husband's February 19, 2019 Complaint for Contempt, and finding Husband not in contempt on Wife's March 7, 2019 Complaint for Contempt.

79. On April 22, 2019, Husband filed a Complaint for Contempt seeking reimbursement for the attorney's fees he paid to Wife in the amount of $25,000 as said order was vacated by the Appeals Court. As of the date of the filing of this Complaint for Contempt, the Court had not issued any order requiring Wife to reimburse Husband for the $25,000 in attorney's fees he paid to her pursuant to the Judgment of Divorce. Accordingly, the Court shall enter a Judgment finding Wife not in contempt. As described above, the Court does not find that either party provided sufficient evidence to warrant an award of attorney's fees in the divorce

matter. Accordingly, in the Judgment on Remand, the Court shall order Wife to reimburse Husband regarding payment of same.

RATIONALE AND FURTHER FINDINGS

On March 7, 2016, the Appeals Court entered the following: "So much of the judgment dated July 8, 2013, that orders division of property is vacated, and that matter is remanded to the Probate and Family Court for further proceedings and findings, and if appropriate, redistribution of the property consistent with this memorandum and order. So much of the judgment that orders attorney's fees is vacated, and that matter is remanded for further proceedings and findings consistent with this memorandum and order. So much of the judgment that orders the husband to pay child support from May, 2011, to the date of trial is vacated. In all other respects, the judgment dated July 8, 2013, is affirmed. The judgment dated December 12, 2013, is affirmed. The order dated January 29, 2014, awarding the wife attorney's fees is vacated."

As described above, the Court does not find that either party provided sufficient evidence to warrant an award of attorney's fees in the divorce matter. Accordingly, the only issue remaining on remand is the division of property.

Property Division

In determining the appropriate division of the marital estate, the Court considered all of the mandatory and discretionary factors of Section 34. At the time of the Judgment of Divorce, the parties were married for 19.25 years. Both parties contributed equally to the marriage. They both worked full-time from the start of the marriage until September of 1998. At that time, Wife began working three and a half days per week so she could be more available to care for Sepideh and Husband. The parties lived an upper-middle-income lifestyle during the marriage, owning their own business, owning several real properties, and sending their daughter to private elementary and middle school. Wife is in good health and has the ability to acquire future assets and income through practicing dentistry. While Husband suffers from MS, he maintains that he also has the ability to acquire future assets and income through practicing dentistry as well as receiving social security disability income and private disability income.

The Court finds that in light of all of the factors set forth in G. L. c. 208, § 34, an approximately equal division of the marital estate is most equitable. In the Judgment of Divorce, the Court (Phelan, J.) awarded each of the parties his or her own bank and retirement accounts. Since that time, the parties have invested and spent his or her own funds as they see fit. Accordingly, the Court finds it equitable to award each party his or her own financial and retirement accounts. Given the fact that the parties' dental office was modified to accommodate Husband's needs, the Court finds it equitable to award Husband Units 102/103, the units in which the dental office is located. In its Judgment, the Court made the following division of the parties' real properties:

Asset	Value at Divorce	Husband's Share	Wife's Share
99 Pond Avenue Unit 406	$357,923		$357,923
77 Pond Avenue Units 102/103	$660,000	$660,000	

77 Pond Avenue Unit 201	$525,000	$525,000	
77 Pond Avenue Unit 406	$390,000	$390,000	
33 Pond Avenue Unit 1008	$305,000		$305,000
Total	**$2,237,923**	**$1,575,000**	**$662,923**

In order to effectuate an equal division of the assets listed above, Husband would be required to pay to Wife $456,038.50. However, that sum shall be reduced by the $25,000 attorney's fees payment Wife must return to Husband. Accordingly, Husband shall pay to Wife $431,038.50 within six months of the date of the Judgment on Remand. If Husband does not timely make said payment to Wife, the parties shall retain the properties they were awarded in the Judgment of Divorce and Unit 1008 shall be placed on the market for sale; the net proceeds to be divided equally. In that case, Wife's 50% share of the net proceeds shall be reduced by $76,461.50, (i.e. $51,461.50 in order to effectuate an equal division of the other properties and reimbursement to Husband for the $25,000 attorney's fees payment).

Date: 8/12/20

Paul M. Cronan, Justice
Norfolk Probate and Family Court

COMMONWEALTH OF MASSACHUSETTS
THE TRIAL COURT
PROBATE AND FAMILY COURT DEPARTMENT

Norfolk Division   Docket No. 11D0426

Kayoko Obara,
Plaintiff

v.

Javad Ghoreishi,
Defendant

JUDGMENT
(On Wife's Complaint for Contempt filed 9/2/14)

This matter came before the Court (Cronan, J.) for a trial on the merits on January 8 and 14, 2020. Kayoko Obara (hereinafter referred to as "Wife") was present and represented by Attorney John B. Jenney. Jr. Javad Ghoreishi (hereinafter referred to as "Husband") was present and proceeded *pro se*. One exhibit was entered into evidence and the following four (4) witnesses testified at trial: Attorney Pasquale DeSantis; Husband; Wife; and Attorney Michael J. Traft. In addition to the one exhibit that was entered at trial, the Court also took judicial notice of the file and the parties' most recent financial statements, Wife's financial statement filed on July 30, 2019 and Husband's financial statement filed on January 14, 2020.

After trial, and consideration of the evidence and all reasonable inferences drawn therefrom, the Court hereby enters the following:

1. Husband is not in contempt.

Date: 8/12/20

_____
Paul M. Cronan, Justice
Norfolk Probate and Family Court

140

COMMONWEALTH OF MASSACHUSETTS
THE TRIAL COURT
PROBATE AND FAMILY COURT DEPARTMENT

Norfolk Division   Docket No. 11D0426

Kayoko Obara,
Plaintiff/Defendant-in-Counterclaim

v.

Javad Ghoreishi,
Defendant Plaintiff-in-Counterclaim

FURTHER JUDGMENT
(On Wife's Complaint for Contempt filed 12/5/14)
(On Husband's Counterclaim for Contempt filed 12/19/14)

This matter came before the Court (Cronan, J.) for a trial on the merits on January 8 and 14, 2020. Kayoko Obara (hereinafter referred to as "Wife") was present and represented by Attorney John B. Jenney, Jr. Javad Ghoreishi (hereinafter referred to as "Husband") was present and proceeded *pro se*. One exhibit was entered into evidence and the following four (4) witnesses testified at trial: Attorney Pasquale DeSantis; Husband; Wife; and Attorney Michael J. Traft. In addition to the one exhibit that was entered at trial, the Court also took judicial notice of the file and the parties' most recent financial statements. Wife's financial statement filed on July 30, 2019 and Husband's financial statement filed on January 14, 2020.

After trial, and consideration of the evidence and all reasonable inferences drawn therefrom, the Court hereby enters the following:

1. Husband is not in contempt except as provided in the Court's February 23, 2015 Partial Judgment.

2. Wife is not in contempt.

Date: 8/12/20

Paul M. Cronan, Justice
Norfolk Probate and Family Court

COMMONWEALTH OF MASSACHUSETTS
THE TRIAL COURT
PROBATE AND FAMILY COURT DEPARTMENT

Norfolk Division   Docket No. 11D0426

Kayoko Obara.
Plaintiff

v.

Javad Ghoreishi,
Defendant

JUDGMENT
(On Wife's Complaint for Contempt filed 3/29/16)

This matter came before the Court (Cronan, J.) for a trial on the merits on January 8 and 14, 2020. Kayoko Obara (hereinafter referred to as "Wife") was present and represented by Attorney John B. Jenney, Jr. Javad Ghoreishi (hereinafter referred to as "Husband") was present and proceeded *pro se*. One exhibit was entered into evidence and the following four (4) witnesses testified at trial: Attorney Pasquale DeSantis; Husband; Wife; and Attorney Michael J. Traft. In addition to the one exhibit that was entered at trial, the Court also took judicial notice of the file and the parties' most recent financial statements, Wife's financial statement filed on July 30, 2019 and Husband's financial statement filed on January 14, 2020.

After trial, and consideration of the evidence and all reasonable inferences drawn therefrom, the Court hereby enters the following:

1. Husband is not in contempt.

Date: 8/12/20

Paul M. Cronan, Justice
Norfolk Probate and Family Court

142

COMMONWEALTH OF MASSACHUSETTS
THE TRIAL COURT
PROBATE AND FAMILY COURT DEPARTMENT

Norfolk Division   Docket No. 11D0426

Javad Ghoreishi,
Plaintiff

v.

Kayoko Obara,
Defendant

JUDGMENT
(On Husband's Complaint for Contempt filed 1/12/18)

This matter came before the Court (Cronan, J.) for a trial on the merits on January 8 and 14, 2020. Kayoko Obara (hereinafter referred to as "Wife") was present and represented by Attorney John B. Jenney, Jr. Javad Ghoreishi (hereinafter referred to as "Husband") was present and proceeded *pro se*. One exhibit was entered into evidence and the following four (4) witnesses testified at trial: Attorney Pasquale DeSantis; Husband; Wife; and Attorney Michael J. Traft. In addition to the one exhibit that was entered at trial, the Court also took judicial notice of the file and the parties' most recent financial statements. Wife's financial statement filed on July 30, 2019 and Husband's financial statement filed on January 14, 2020.

After trial, and consideration of the evidence and all reasonable inferences drawn therefrom, the Court hereby enters the following:

1. Wife is not in contempt.

Date: __8/12/20__   _____
                                     Paul M. Cronan, Justice
                                     Norfolk Probate and Family Court

143

COMMONWEALTH OF MASSACHUSETTS
THE TRIAL COURT
PROBATE AND FAMILY COURT DEPARTMENT

Norfolk Division   **Docket No. 11D0426**

Javad Ghoreishi,
Plaintiff

v.

Kayoko Obara,
Defendant

JUDGMENT
(On Husband's Complaint for Contempt filed 2/19/19)

This matter came before the Court (Cronan, J.) for a trial on the merits on January 8 and 14, 2020. Kayoko Obara (hereinafter referred to as "Wife") was present and represented by Attorney John B. Jenney, Jr. Javad Ghoreishi (hereinafter referred to as "Husband") was present and proceeded *pro se*. One exhibit was entered into evidence and the following four (4) witnesses testified at trial: Attorney Pasquale DeSantis; Husband; Wife; and Attorney Michael J. Traft. In addition to the one exhibit that was entered at trial, the Court also took judicial notice of the file and the parties' most recent financial statements, Wife's financial statement filed on July 30, 2019 and Husband's financial statement filed on January 14, 2020.

After trial, and consideration of the evidence and all reasonable inferences drawn therefrom, the Court hereby enters the following:

1. Wife is not in contempt.

Date: 8/12/20

_____
Paul M. Cronan, Justice
Norfolk Probate and Family Court

144

COMMONWEALTH OF MASSACHUSETTS
THE TRIAL COURT
PROBATE AND FAMILY COURT DEPARTMENT

Norfolk Division   Docket No. 11D0426

Kayoko Obara,
Plaintiff

v.

Javad Ghoreishi,
Defendant

JUDGMENT
(On Wife's Complaint for Contempt filed 3/7/19)

This matter came before the Court (Cronan, J.) for a trial on the merits on January 8 and 14, 2020. Kayoko Obara (hereinafter referred to as "Wife") was present and represented by Attorney John B. Jenney, Jr. Javad Ghoreishi (hereinafter referred to as "Husband") was present and proceeded *pro se*. One exhibit was entered into evidence and the following four (4) witnesses testified at trial: Attorney Pasquale DeSantis; Husband; Wife; and Attorney Michael J. Traft. In addition to the one exhibit that was entered at trial, the Court also took judicial notice of the file and the parties' most recent financial statements. Wife's financial statement filed on July 30, 2019 and Husband's financial statement filed on January 14, 2020.

After trial, and consideration of the evidence and all reasonable inferences drawn therefrom, the Court hereby enters the following:

1. Husband is not in contempt.

Date: __8/12/20__

Paul M. Cronan, Justice
Norfolk Probate and Family Court

145

Tracer: 18053713 - Amt: $10,000.00 - 07/19/2013   Tracer: 18053713 - Amt: $10,000.00 - 07/19/2013

Tracer: 18057012 - Amt: $10,000.00 - 08/01/2013   Tracer: 18057012 - Amt: $10,000.00 - 08/01/2013

Tracer: 18076820 - Amt: $40,446.00 - 08/20/2013   Tracer: 18076820 - Amt: $40,446.00 - 08/20/2013

Tracer: 18100791 - Amt: $3,000.00 - 10/08/2013   Tracer: 18100791 - Amt: $3,000.00 - 10/08/2013

JAVAD GHOREISHI, D.M.D.
77 POND AVE APT 103
BROOKLINE, MA 02445

53-179/113

1139

DATE Oct. 5, 2013

PAY TO THE ORDER OF Fent + Glazer $3,000.00

Three Thousand and no/100 DOLLARS

⊘ Eastern Bank
Boston, MA 02110
easternbank.com
1-800-EASTERN

MEMO Legal fees

⑈011301798⑈ 04 0514488⑈ 1139

Tracer: 18100791 - Amt: $3,000.00 - 10/08/2013

Tracer: 18100791 - Amt: $3,000.00 - 10/08/2013

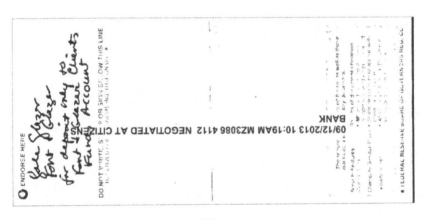

JAVAD GHOREISHI, D.M.D.
77 POND AVE APT 103
BROOKLINE, MA 02445

53-179/113   1138

DATE Sept. 11, 2013

PAY TO THE ORDER OF Font & Glazer $ 7,000.—

Seven thousand and NO/100   DOLLARS

Eastern Bank Boston, MA 02110
easternbank.com
1-800-EASTERN

MEMO   MP

⑈011301798⑈ 04 05144882⑈ 1138

Tracer: 18058241 - Amt: $7,000.00 - 09/13/2013

ENDORSE HERE

Font & Glazer
for deposit only to
Font & Glazer Clients
Funds Account

DO NOT WRITE, STAMP OR SIGN BELOW THIS LINE

09/12/2013 10:19AM MZ3086 4112 NEGOTIATED AT CITIZENS BANK

* FEDERAL RESERVE BOARD OF GOVERNORS REG. CC

Tracer: 18058241 - Amt: $7,000.00 - 09/13/2013

JAVAD GHOREISHI, D.M.D.
77 POND AVE APT 103
BROOKLINE, MA 02445

53-179/113

1137

DATE Aug- 17, 2013

PAY TO THE ORDER OF Font & Glazer — $40,446

Forty thousand four hundred forty-six and NO/100 DOLLARS

⊘Eastern Bank
Boston, MA 02110
easternbank.com
1-800-EASTERN

MEMO fees

⑆011301798⑆ 04 0514488 2⑈ 1137

Tracer: 18076820 - Amt: $40,446.00 - 08/20/2013

Tracer: 18076820 - Amt: $40,446.00 - 08/20/2013

149

Tracer: 18057012 - Amt: $10,000.00 - 08/01/2013

Tracer: 18057012 - Amt: $10,000.00 - 08/01/2013

JAVAD GHOREISHI, D.M.D.
77 POND AVE APT 103
BROOKLINE, MA 02445

53-175/113

1130

DATE 7/18/13

PAY TO THE ORDER OF Font + Glazer Clients Funds $ 10,000 $\frac{00}{100}$

Acct.

Ten Thousand only ————— DOLLARS

⊘ **Eastern Bank** Boston, MA 02110
eastembank.com
1-800-EASTERN

MEMO Partial retainel

⑆011301798⑆ 04 0514488 2⑈ 1130

Tracer: 18053713 - Amt: $10,000.00 - 07/19/2013

for deposit only to
Font + Glazer
Clients Funds Account
Lynne Frost

Tracer: 18053713 - Amt: $10,000.00 - 07/19/2013

JAVAD S GHOREISHI
77 POND AVE STE 103
BROOKLINE MA 02446-7115

102

53-13/110 MA
81220

August 3, 2013
Date

Pay to the
Order of _Font + Glazer_ $5,000.⁰⁰

—Five Thousand and ⁿᵒ/₁₀₀ —————Dollars

Bank of America

ACH R/T 011000138

For _Final payment on_
Initial retainer

⑈011000138⑈ 004637678173⑈0102

08/04/2013 02:29PM MZ3086 8189 NEGOTIATED AT CITIZENS BANK

Font + Glazer
...
...
...
...

Electronic Endorsements:

Date	Sequence	Bank #	Endrs Type	TRN	RRC	Bank Name
08/04/2013	000009200461694	11500120	Rtn Loc/BOFD	Y		CITIZENS BANK, NA
08/06/2013	006092790585	111012822	Pay Bank	N		BANK OF AMERICA, NA

Commonwealth of Massachusetts
Executive Office of Health and Human Services
Department of Public Health
Bureau of Health Professions Licensure
Board of Registration in Dentistry
239 Causeway Street, Suite 500, Boston, MA 02114

CHARLES D. BAKER
Governor

KARYN E. POLITO
Lieutenant Governor

Tel: 617-973-0971
Fax : 617-973-0980
TTY : 617-973-0988
www.mass.gov/dph/boards/dn

MARYLOU SUDDERS
Secretary

MONICA BHAREL, MD, MPH
Commissioner

March 29, 2017

By first-class mail
Michael J. Traft, Esq.
One State Street, Suite 1500
Boston, MA 02109

RE: **In the Matter of Dr. Javad Ghoreishi, DN18050**
      Docket No. DEN-2016-0083

Dear Attorney Traft:

As you know, the Board of Registration in Dentistry ("Board") reviewed the complaint identified above and determined additional evaluation is needed and is offering Dr. Ghoreishi a one year stayed probation disposition. *A stayed probation is a non-disciplinary disposition, which is not reported to the National Practitioner Data Bank.*

Enclosed please find a Consent Agreement for Stayed Probation ("Agreement") for your client to consider. If Dr. Ghoreishi decides to execute the Agreement, the Board will impose a one year Stayed Probation against your client's dental license and agree to refrain from further action related to the complaint. The Agreement is a final action and should be considered carefully.

If Dr. Ghoreishi wishes to enter into the Agreement with the Board, please have him sign and return both originals to me at your earliest convenience but no later than **April 19, 2017**. The Board's Executive Director will then sign each and an executed original will be returned to you for your client's records. Please do not fax or send a copy of the signed Agreement; the Board will only accept an Agreement with an original signature.

If you wish to request a hearing on this matter, please notify the Board by April 19, 2017. If Dr. Goreishi fails to request a hearing or execute the Agreement, the Board will issue an Order to Show Cause, requiring Dr. Ghoreshi to demonstrate at an administrative hearing why the Board should not take appropriate disciplinary action against his dental license.

Thank you for your cooperation in this matter. If you have any questions, please contact me at (617) 973-0950.

Sincerely,

Samuel Leadholm, Board Counsel
Board of Registration in Dentistry

Encl.

SWL/*lf*

COMMONWEALTH OF MASSACHUSETTS

SUFFOLK COUNTY

BOARD OF REGISTRATION
IN DENTISTRY

In the Matter of Dr. Javad Ghoreishi License No. DN18050 Expires March 31, 2018	Docket No. DEN-2016-0083

CONSENT AGREEMENT FOR STAYED PROBATION

The Massachusetts Board of Registration in Dentistry ("Board") and Dr. Javad Ghoreishi ("Licensee"), license[1] no. DN18050 ("License") do hereby stipulate and agree the following information shall be entered into and become a permanent part of the Licensee's record maintained by the Board:

1. The Licensee hereby states that he voluntarily enters into this Consent Agreement for Stayed Probation ("Agreement") in order to resolve the allegations of the Complaint pending against his License before the Board at docket no. DEN-2016-0083 (hereinafter, the "Complaint").

2. The Licensee and the Board stipulate and agree to resolve the Complaint without making any findings and without proceeding to a formal adjudicatory hearing on the Complaint.

3. The Licensee and the Board acknowledge the Agreement is a non-disciplinary agreement not reported to the National Practitioner Data Bank or other outside reporting agencies, except that the Licensee's failure to fulfill the requirements of paragraph 5 may result in the imposition of discipline by the Board.

4. In order to resolve the Complaint without further proceedings before the Board, the Licensee and the Board agree on the date the Board executes the Agreement ("Effective Date"), the Board will order the Licensee be placed on Probation for one year, and the Probation Order will be Stayed for one year ("Stayed Probation" or "Stayed Probation Period") from the Effective Date.

5. Within the Stayed Probation Period, the Licensee shall submit his practice of dentistry to an evaluation by a Board-approved licensed dentist to assess a Boad-approved dental procedure to determine whether or not Licensee is fit to practice

---

[1] The term "license" or "License" applies to both a current and expired license as well as the right to renew an expired license.

dentistry, as follows:

(a) Within 60 days of the Effective Date, the Licensee shall provide the Board the names and curricula vitae of at least two licensed dentists who are not related professionally or otherwise to Licensee and have: (1) read this Agreement; (2) agree to evaluate the Licensee's practice of dentistry of a least one Board-aproved dental procedure; and (3) thereafter agree to submit a written evaluation directly to the Board of Licensee's practice of dentistry (hereinafter "Evaluation").

(b) At the same time the Licensee submits information related to 5(a), he shall submit to the Board a list of three dental procedures he would typically perform.

(c) The Board will review (a) and (b) and determine who will evaluate what dental procedure to be performed by the Licensee.

(d) The Board will review the Evaluation and determine whether or not Licensee is fit to practice dentistry.

   1. If the Board determines Licensee is fit to practice dentistry after reviewing the Evaluation, the complaint will be dismissed without prejudice.

   2. If the Board determines Licensee is not fit to practice dentistry, it will determine what License restrictions are necessary for the protection of the public health, safety and welfare; such restrictions shall be imposed either after obtaining Licensee's written consent or a final decision and order issued pursuant to M.G.L. c. 30A and the Standard Adjudicatory Rules of Practice and Procedure, 801 CMR 1.01 and 1.03

   3. If the Board is unable to determine Licensee's fitness to practice dentistry from the Evaluation, Licensee will submit to further dental practice evaluation.

(e) Licensee has the burden to prove compliance with the requirements of the Agreement.

6. If the Licensee successfully completes the requirements of paragraph 5 within the Stayed Probation Period, his License will not be placed on probation. The Licensee may terminate the Stayed Probation Period and his obligations under the Agreement sooner by submitting a written request with documentation demonstrating successful completion of the requirements of paragraph 5.

7. If the Licensee fails to successfully complete the requirements of paragraph 5, the Stay may be withdrawn by the Board and the Board's order of Probation for one year ("Probation" or "Probation Period") will be imposed upon the Licensee

2

without a hearing. During the Probation Period, the following terms and conditions shall be imposed:

(a) Licensee's practice of dentistry shall be monitored. Licensee shall submit to Board the names and curricula vitae of at least two licensed dentists who are not related to the Licensee, professionally or otherwise, and have read this agreement, agree to monitor Licensee's practice of dentistry in a manner determined by the Board and agree to submit monthly written reports to the Board. Licensee agrees to bear all costs associated with having his dental practice monitored.

(b) The Licensee shall successfully pass the *Massachusetts Dental Ethics and Jurisprudence Examination* within 30 days from the date the Board withdraws the Stay of Probation.

(c) Within 30 days from the date the Board withdraws the Stay of Probation, Licensee shall inform all jurisdictions in which he holds a license to practice dentistry that his License has been placed on Probation.

    (i) Licensee shall provide written documentation to the Board demonstrating his compliance with paragraph 7(c).

    (ii) If Licensee is not licensed to practice dentistry or another health profession in any other jurisdiction, he shall submit a signed attestation to the Board stating such.

(d) The Licensee has the burden to prove compliance with the requirements of the Agreement.

8. If the Licensee fails to successfully complete the requirements of paragraph 7 or engage in the unmonitoried practice of dentistry, the Board shall take further disciplinary action. Such action may include, but not be limited to, extension of the Probation Period, suspension of his License, suspension of the right to renew his License or other disciplinary action as deemed appropriate by the Board.

9. During either the Stayed Probation Period or the Probation Period, the Licensee further agrees he shall not:

(a) Violate any state or federal law or regulation relating to the practice of dentistry, and

(b) Commit any act that constitutes deceit, malpractice, gross misconduct in the practice of dentistry, unprofessional conduct, or conduct which undermines public confidence in the integrity of the profession.

(c) The Licensee agrees to fully cooperate and respond to any inquiry or request

3

made by the Board pursuant to M.G.L. c. 112, § 43 and 234 CMR 2.00 *et seq.*

(d) The Licensee has the burden to prove compliance with the requirements of the Agreement.

10. The Licensee agrees his failure to satisfy any of the terms in paragraph 9 shall result in further disciplinary action by the Board pursuant to subparagraphs 10(a) & (b).

(a) The Licensee shall be entitled to a hearing as to whether he violated any condition in paragraph 10 of the Agreement. This hearing shall be conducted in accordance with the State Administrative Procedure Act, M.G.L. c. 30A, §§ 10 and 11, and the Standard Adjudicatory Rules of Practice and Procedure, 801 CMR 1.01 and 1.03.

(b) After a hearing, if the Board determines a violation did occur during the Stayed Probation or Probation Period, it will impose a further sanction deemed appropriate in its sole discretion.

(c) The Licensee agrees he is not entitled to a hearing to dispute the Complaint or the sanction to be imposed upon a finding of failure to comply with the terms of his Probation. The Licensee agrees by entering into the Agreement, he is relinquishing important procedural rights.

11. The Licensee acknowledges entering into the Agreement is a final act and not subject to reconsideration, collateral attack or judicial review in any form or forum.

12. The Licensee acknowledges and understands the Agreement is subject to the Commonwealth of Massachusetts' Public Records Law, M.G.L. c. 4, § 7(26).

13. The Board agrees as consideration for the Licensee entering into the Agreement, the Board will forego further prosecution of Complaint's allegations. Any prosecution regarding the Complaint will relate only to whether the Agreement's requirements were violated.

14. The Licensee enters into the Agreement of his own free will. The Licensee is aware he has a right to counsel in this matter and has either conferred with counsel prior to signing the Agreement or waives his right to counsel.

15. A waiver by the Board of any provision of the Agreement at any time shall not constitute a waiver of any other provision of the Agreement, nor shall it constitute a waiver by the Board of its right to enforce such provision at any future time.

16. The Licensee has read the Agreement. The Licensee understands he has the right to a formal adjudicatory hearing concerning the allegations set forth in the Complaint and that at a hearing he would have the right to confront and cross-examine witnesses, call witnesses, present evidence, testify on his own behalf, contest the

4

allegations, present oral argument, seek judicial review and to all other rights set forth in the State Administrative Procedure Act, M.G. L. c. 30A, and 801 CMR 1.00 *et seq.* By executing the Agreement, Licensee knowingly and voluntarily waives his right to a formal adjudicatory hearing and to all of the above-enumerated rights set forth in the State Administrative Procedure Act, M.G.L. c. 30A and 801 CMR 1.00 *et seq.*, except as provided in subparagraph 10(a) & (b).

Licensee

_____   _____
Dr. Javad Ghoreishi   Date Signed

Board of Registration in Dentistry

_____   _____
Barbara A. Young, RDH   Date Signed
Executive Director

                                        _____
                                        Effective Date

5

FORM BBO-1
Page One

OFFICE OF THE BAR COUNSEL
OF THE
BOARD OF BAR OVERSEERS
OF THE SUPREME JUDICIAL COURT
FOR THE
COMMONWEALTH OF MASSACHUSETTS

REQUEST FOR INVESTIGATION

Date __11/15/2014__

Instructions:

(1)   Please type, if possible. Otherwise use a dark pen.

(2)   Write only on the front side of the paper.

(3)   Specify exactly what the attorney did that you believe to have been misconduct.

(4)   Attach additional sheets, if necessary, as well as copies of any documents which will help explain the facts. Please do not send original documents.

(5)   Retain copies for your records of this and any subsequent correspondence and documentation sent to this office.

(6)   Please return to:

OFFICE OF THE BAR COUNSEL
99 High Street
Boston, Massachusetts 02110
(617) 728-8750
http://www.state.ma.us/obcbbo/

1.   I, __JAVAD GHOREISHI__ ,

     (type or print your full name)

allege that attorney __Pasquale Desantis__ ,

whose office address is __100 Cambridge Street, suite 2250, Boston, MA, 02114__

has committed acts of misconduct as set forth in the Statement of Facts attached.

2.   I request that the Office of the Bar Counsel investigate this misconduct.

3.   I understand that a copy of this statement may be mailed to the attorney for a reply.

4.   I understand that this matter must be kept confidential by Bar Counsel and the Board of Bar Overseers.

(signature) __J. Ghoreishi__

(address) __77 Pond Ave # 201__

          __Brookline, MA 02445__

(telephone):   Work __612 651-1500__

          Home __617-651-1500__

PLEASE USE ATTACHED SHEET FOR STATEMENT

160

FORM BBO-1
Page Two

STATEMENT OF FACTS

Please do not write above this line and write only on the front of this and any other pages you attach.

Please fill in the following, if applicable:

Court case name: Rayoko Obara vs. Javad Shoreishi

Name of Court: Probat and Family Court Dept Norfolk county

Court case number: Docket No. 11 D 0426

Statement of Facts:

According to the attached Judment decree on 7/5/13 residential unit of C 201 at 77 Pond Ave #201 was given to husband Javad Ghoreishi.

On Feb, 04, 2014 a deed submited to Registry of deed That on that deed (affeen) husband (Javad Ghoreishi) signiture is forged and Attorney Pasquale Desantis' Neutary seal of approval is on that Deed. This fraudent deed has been submited to Registry of deed on Feb. 4, 2014.

Husband, Javad Ghoreishi di covered this fraudent deed on 10/24 when he went to pay his property (unit C201 at 77 Pond Ave). Sine his discovery of this fraudelent actions husband who is wheelchair bound due to multiple Sclerosis (MS) he is b. in a great stressful situation and having sleepless nights and he is endoring great pain and suffering from created fraudelent situatio A Torney General als hasbeen notified from this fraudelent acting

Division of Neutary Public of The Secretary of state was also been notify from This activity

I would like To bring The fact That I have Contested The Judgment and This Case is already been docketed in apalete court REF No 2014-P-1746

FEE AGREEMENT

PARTIES: Kayoko Obara v. Javad Ghoreishi / Norfolk Probate and Family Court,
            Docket No. 11D0426

MATTER: Special Master for Discovery - March 18, 2019 Order (Cronan, J.)

Jennifer C. Roman, Esquire (hereinafter "the Attorney") was appointed by the Norfolk County Probate and Family Court on March 18, 2019 as a Discovery Master in the matter of Kayoko Obara v. Javad Ghoreishi. Pursuant to the Order appointing the Attorney as Discovery Master, compensation for this matter will be as follows:

1) A retainer in the amount of $6,000.00 is to be paid by the Parties upon the acceptance of this matter by the Attorney. **The Plaintiff and Defendant shall each pay $3,000.00 towards the initial retainer amount pursuant to the Court's Order.** This payment represents only an estimated partial payment of attorney's fees and costs in this matter. If the retainer is expended, the Parties shall replenish same equally in an amount determined by the Court or by the Attorney. This retainer will be held as trust funds in a client trust account, and earned fees and costs will be withdrawn from the client trust account upon delivering to the Parties in writing (i) an itemized bill or other accounting showing the serviced rendered, (ii) written notice of the amount which shall be withdrawn three (3) days after the date of the notice, unless the Parties object, and (iii) a statement of the balance of the Parties' funds in the trust account after the withdrawal. Unless otherwise agreed upon, bills shall be sent by electronic mail only.

2) Services will be billed monthly by the Attorney to the Parties on the basis of his/her time expended at the rate of $360.00 per hour. It is agreed that said rate shall change effective upon any change in the Attorney's customary hourly rate.

3) In addition to any retainer fee and hourly rate fees, the Parties shall reimburse the Attorney for such reasonable costs, disbursements, filing fees, travel expenses, long

distance calls and costs of discovery as the Attorney deems necessary to properly prepare and handle the case.

4) It is understood and agreed that the hourly time charged for legal services includes, but is not limited to, the following: conferences, preparation of pleadings and other documents, court appearances, telephone calls, electronic mail, correspondence, legal research, depositions and other discovery, general research, travel, review of documents, and preparation for hearings. Any telephone calls, correspondence or other time charges will be billed at a minimum of one-tenth (.10) of one hour.

5) In the event that on the completion of the within matter, or the termination of the Attorney's involvement in this matter, if the total cost of the legal services performed by the Attorney shall be less than the amount paid on account by the Parties, the balance shall be refunded to the Parties by the Attorney.

6) The Parties understand and acknowledge that no preparation or work shall begin in this matter until the retainer fee as set forth in Paragraph (1) is paid in full.

7) **This document constitutes the entire agreement concerning fees between the parties, who acknowledge that they have read the document before signing and acknowledge receipt of a duplicate copy of this Fee Agreement. This is a legally binding contract. Ask to have any term that you do not fully understand explained to you so you completely understand this Agreement.**

Dated: _____   _____
                                  Kayoko Obara

                                  _____
                                  Javad Ghoreishi

                                  HOFFMAN LAW GROUP

                                  By: _____
                                      Jennifer C. Roman, Esquire

Itemization

Date	Work Performed	Time	
7/17/13	GG & LF: Conf. with client	2.0	
	GG: Rev Findings & Judgment	2.2	
7/18/13	GG: TC with court clerk, Norfolk Probate & Family Court	0.2	
	TCs with Atty. Helman	0.4	
	TC w/Steve Shama	0.2	NC
	LF: review of 300+ Findings	3.0	
	GG & LF: Conf. with client	0.9	
	GG & LF: Travel from client's home to Atty. Helman's office in Newton, MA, and from Newton, MA to F & G office in Boston	1.3	0.6 NC
	GG & LF: Conf. with Atty. Helman And rec from him one box of documents which he said was the entire file	0.4	
	GG & LF: Begin review of client file, including post trial submissions by client and by mother; Continue legal research re: whether in best interest of client to file a motion for a new trial and or a motion to amend the findings	5.8	
	GG: Draft fee agreement; Draft email to client with attached agreement	1.0	NC
7/19/13	GG & LF: legal research re post-trial motions and advisability of filing same; TCs with client; Continue review of client's file; Review trial exhibits found in the file; Legal Research re: stay pending appeal	4.5	
	GG & LF: Conf. with client	1.3	

1

	LF: Draft emails to client	0.5	
	GG: TC w/Clerk, Norfolk Probate & Family Court	0.2	
	TC to Client, lft vm	0.1	NC
	GG & LF: review documents from client's file; Continue review of Findings and Judgment; Legal research re appellate issues, etc.	5.5	
	GG: Research	1.3	
7/20/13	GG & LF Confs. with client; Conf. w/Steve Shama	7.0	
7/21/13	GG & LF: Confs. with client; Conf. w/Steve Shama	5.4	
	LF: Review client's deposition	1.0	
7/22/13	LF: continue review of client's deposition; review trial exhibits	2.2	
	LF: Legal research	4.5	
	GG: TC with client	0.1	
	Further review of Findings; legal research	4.2	
7/23/13	LF: Review client files received from Atty. Helman	1.0	
	LF: begin draft of motion for emergency stay and memorandum of law in support, for submission to the trial judge; legal research; Begin draft of chronology taken from trial exhibits, Findings, and Judgment	9.0	
	GG: Rec and rev email from Dr. Houtchens; draft email to Dr. Houtchens; TC w/Dr.. Houtchens; draft affidavit	1.5	
	TC w/Client	0.2	
	TC to Client, lft vm	0.1	NC
	Research	1.2	
7/24/13	LF: draft memorandum of law for trial judge; legal research; draft chronology	8.5	
	GG: Rev emails from Dr. Houtchens; Draft emails to		

2

	Dr. Houtchens	0.2	
	TCs w/Client	0.3	
	Legal Research	5.2	
	TC w/Steve Shama	0.4	
	TC w/possible witness	0.1	

7/25/13   LF: draft memorandum of law for trial
judge; legal research   7.5

GG: TC w/Client	0.1	
Legal Research	4.7	
Draft affidavit of Steve Shama, and draft email to him	1.1	
TC to Ray Rezania, left vm	0.1	NC
Draft email to Client	0.1	NC

7/26/13   LF: Draft pleadings for stay for submission to
the trial court; Legal research   12.0

         GG: rec and rev email from Client   0.1

7/27/13   GG & LF: Draft pleadings for submission to
the trial court; Legal research   12.0

7/28/13   GG & LF: Conf. w/Client; Conf. w/Ray Rezania;
Draft pleadings for submission to
the trial court; Legal research; redraft affidavit of client;
Draft affidavit of Ray Rezania; Draft affidavit of Atty.
Glazer; Draft Notice of Appeal   12.0

7/29/1   GG: Draft and finalize pleadings to file at Norfolk
Probate & Family Court   4.5
Redraft and email to Client his affidavit   0.4
Draft correspondence to Atty. Medonis   0.1

GG & LF: Travel to and from Boston to
Norfolk Probate & Family Court, Canton, MA.   1.8   0.9 NC

GG: Conferences with court clerks at
Norfolk Family and Probate Court; file
Defendant's Emergency Motion for Stay
(ex parte); Review trial judge's decision
denying same; draft and file
motion for short order of notice;
review order of trial judge denying same;
order CDs of trial; obtain certified

3

copy of court docket, date stamped copy
of pleadings filed this date, date stamped
copies of trial judge's decisions this date;
TC with client   1.6

      EXP – Payment for CDs $155.00

GG: Draft Motion for Emergency Stay
to the Appeals Court; supporting Memorandum;
legal research re same   8.0

LF: Draft emails to client with attached Docket   .5   NC
Sheets obtained today; Judge's rulings this date;
motion for stay and memorandum as filed before
the trial Court today

7/30/13   GG: TC w/Appeals Court clerk;
Legal research and draft pleadings for the
Appeals Court; Draft motion for emergency stay;
Draft memorandum in support; Legal research   14.0
Draft 2 emails to Atty. Medonis   0.2
Rev emails from Atty. Medonis   0.1

LF: Revise memorandum of law
for submission to the Appeals
Court; draft and compile Addendum to
Motion for Emergency Stay before the Appeals
Court; draft and compile Record
Appendix to accompany Memorandum
to the Appeals Court; review and revise
pleadings   14.0

LF: TC to client re status of case   0.2

7/31/13   GG: File at the Appeals Court
the following: Emergency Motion for
Stay, Addendum to Motion, Memorandum of
Law in support of emergency stay;
Record Appendix to accompany Memorandum
of Law in Support of Stay; Obtain date-stamped
copies of pleadings   0.5

      EXP – Appeals Ct. Filing Fee $315.00

GG: Draft emails to Appeals Court to E-file

4

	all pleadings	0.2	
	LF: serve copies of Appeals Court pleadings by hand delivery to Kayoko's counsel	0.4	NC
	EXP – Center Plaza Parking $14.00		
	GG: TCs with Appeals Court clerks, stay granted; Review fax received from court clerk; Draft fax to Atty. Medonis with Appeals Court order granting Temporary Stay	0.6	
	EXP – FAX $2.00		
	GG: TCs with client re status of case; Draft email to opposing counsel; Draft emails to client; LF: Draft email to client	0.9	
	GG: Draft emails to client with pleadings provided to the Appeals Court; TCs with client	1.0	
	GG & LF: Meet with client in the evening	1.5	NC
8/1/13	GG & LF: Receive and review hand-delivered copy of Kayoko's Opposition submitted to the Appeals Court by Kayoko's counsel on 7/31/13	0.5	
	LF: Draft emails to client with attached copies of Appeals Court Notice of Docket Entry, and Kayoko's Opposition	0.1	NC
8/2/13	GG: Review email from Client; TC w/Client re same	0.2	
8/3/13	GG & LF: Conf. with client	2.0	
8/5/13	GG: TC w/Client TC to Client Rev email from Dr. Houtchens; TC w/Dr. Houtchens Rec and rev Appearance of Atty. Xavier	0.1 0.1 0.1 0.1	 NC NC
8/6/13	GG: TC w/Client Draft email to Atty. Xavier Draft email to Client	0.1 0.1 0.1	 NC
8/8/13	GG: Conf. with client; Conf. with Steve Shama	1.3	NC

5

8/9/13	GG & LF: Receive and review 2nd Docket Entry (order) from Appeals Court and discuss		0.5	
	GG: TC w/Appeals Court clerk		0.1	NC
	TC w/Client		0.2	
	TC to Norfolk Probate Court; TCs re transcription of CDs	0.5	NC	
	LF: Draft email to client with attachment (new Appeals Court order); TC with client		0.2	
8/10/13	GG & LF: Conf w/Client; see dental office		3.0	
	GG: rev file		0.4	
8/11/13	GG: TC w/Client		0.1	
	TC to witness, lft vm		0.1	NC

Total hours	193.0
Minus Hours Not Charged (NC)	7.4
Total	185.6

Legal fee is 185.6 hours x $350/hour which is		$64,960
Expenses Expenses		
Payment for Trial CDs (from Clients' Funds)		$155.00
Appeals Court Filing Fee (from Clients' Funds)	+	$315.00
Parking	+	$ 14.00
Fax	+	$ 2.00
		$486.00

Total Fees Plus Expenses:	$65,446

Amount paid:

7/18/13		$10,000
7/28/13	+	$10,000
8/2/13	+	$ 5,000
Total	=	$25,000

Balance Due	$40,446

6

<u>Javad Ghoreishi, D.M.D.</u>

Itemization
8/11/13 to 10/4/13

<u>Date</u>	<u>Work Performed</u>	<u>Time</u>	
8/11/13	Rec and rev email from witness; draft email to witness	0.1	NC
	Research	0.8	
8/12/13	GG: rec and rev emails from Client	0.2	
	TC w/witness; draft affidavit; draft email to witness; TC w/Brookline Public Health Dept.; rec and rev fax from Brookline Public Health Dept.; TCs w/Client	1.9	
	Rec and rev email from Atty. Medonis	0.1	
8/13/13	GG: Rec and rev affidavit from Witness; draft email to Client	0.2	
	LF: Arrange for and obtain copies of CDs of trial testimony	0.6	NC
	LF: Rev affidavit from witness	0.1	NC
8/14/13	GG: rec and rev email from Client	0.1	
	TCs w/Probate Court	0.3	
	TC to Appeals Clerk at Probate Court, lft vm	0.1	
	Draft fax to Court	0.3	
	EXP – FAX $2.00		
	Draft email to witness	0.1	
8/15/13	GG: TC w/Richard Schmidt of Norfolk Probate & Family Court	0.1	
	draft emails to Atty. Medonis; rec and rev email from Atty. Medonis	0.1	
	Draft email to Client	0.1	NC
	TC w/Client	0.1	
	Draft fax to Atty. Medonis	0.1	
8/16/13	GG: rec and rev email from Client	0.1	
8/17/13	GG: Conf w/Client (at his home)	3.7	
	LF: Conf w/Client (at his home)	3.7	NC
8/18/13	GG: Conf w/Client (at his home)	2.1	

1

	LF: Conf w/Client (at his home)	2.1	NC
	GG: rev materials provided by Client	2.5	
	LF: rev materials provided by Client	2.5	NC
8/19/13	GG: Draft corresp to Court and email		
	to Atty. Medonis	0.3	
	GG: Listen to trial testimony	1.8	
	LF: Listen to trial testimony	1.8	NC
8/20/13	GG: TC w/Client	0.1	
	GG: Listen to trial testimony	2.0	
	LF: Listen to trial testimony	2.0	NC
8/21/13	GG: Rec and rev Opposition to Motion for Stay		
	Pending Appeal; Prepare for hearing tomorrow	2.6	
8/22/13	GG: Conf w/Client prior to Hearing	2.0	
	Prepare for Hearing	1.5	
	Hearing at Norfolk Probate & Family Court	1.5	
	LF: Conf w/Client prior to Hearing	2.0	NC
	Hearing at Norfolk Probate & Family Court	1.5	NC
	Travel to and from Court	1.5	0.7 NC
8/23/13	GG: Conf w/Client	1.2	
	Research	0.8	
8/24/13	GG: Listen to trial testimony	2.0	
	LF: Listen to trial testimony	2.0	NC
8/25/13	GG: Draft email to Client	0.1	
	GG: Conf w/Client (at his home)	1.5	
	Draft Affidavit	2.1	
	LF: Conf w/Client (at his home)	1.5	NC
	Research	0.7	
8/26/13	GG: draft email to Atty. Medonis	0.1	
	Rec and rev corresp from Probate Court Appeals		
	Clerk	0.2	
	Research	0.5	
	TCs w/Client	0.4	
	Continue drafting Affidavit	4.9	
8/27/13	GG: TCs w/Client; Finish drafting Client's		
	Affidavit	6.0	
	LF: Rev and assist GG w/Client's Affidavit	4.0	NC
	Draft FAX to Court w/Affidavit (38 pp),		

2

	and FAX to Atty. Medonis		
	EXP - FAX $76.00		
	Rec and rev email from Atty. Medonis	0.1	NC
8/29/13	GG: Prepare for hearing tomorrow	1.1	
	TCs w/Atty. Medonis re continuance		
	On hrg scheduled for tomorrow; TCs w/Client	0.5	
8/30/13	GG: Analyze Court order re payments due		
	today; determine amounts due; TCs w/Client;		
	Draft & revise letter to Atty. Xavier (not sent);		
	Draft email to Client;		
	C w/Client (at his home);		
	Draft letter to Kayoko re pmts due today	3.0	1.0 NC
	LF: C w/Client to obtain checks due today	0.2	
	LF: C w/Client and GG at Client's home	3.0	NC
	Travel to & from Client's home (LF)	1.0	NC
	Travel to & from Client's home (LF & GG)	0.9	NC
9/3/13	GG: Draft transcription form for		
	Cambridge Transcriptions	0.3	0.1 NC
	EXP – FAX to		
	Cambridge Transcriptions $1.00		
	LF: provide data for transcription form	0.4	NC
	Rec and rev scheduling order from Norfolk		
	Probate Court	0.1	NC
9/5/13	GG: Rec and rev scheduling order from Norfolk		
	Probate Court; draft email to Client	0.1	
9/6/13	GG: Go to Cambridge Transcriptions, drop off		
	Disks; discuss transcription for appeal	0.3	
	Travel to & from office	0.8	0.4 NC
	EXP – deposit to Cambridge Transcriptions		
	(pd out of pocket by Atty. Glazer) $100.00		
9/8/13	GG: review Appellate Procedure Rules re form		
	due tomorrow at Probate Court	0.5	
	LF: confer w/GG re form & Appellate Rules	0.5	NC
9/9/13	GG: TC w/Cambridge Transcriptions	0.1	NC
	Complete Appeals Questionnaire and Draft		
	Letter to Probate Court Appeals Clerk	0.6	
	EXP – FAX to Probate Court - $3.00		
	Research	0.7	

3

9/10/13	GG: rev FAX from Cambridge Transcriptions	0.1	NC
	TC w/Probate Court Appeals Clerk	0.5	
	TC w/Client	0.2	
	Prepare for Hearing tomorrow	2.5	

9/11/13   GG: Hearing before Judge Phelan at
Norfolk Probate & Family Court   2.3
LF: Hearing before Judge Phelan at Norfolk
Probate & Family Court   2.3   NC
Travel to & from Court   1.5   0.7 NC

9/17/13   GG: Draft corresp to Probate Court Appeals Clerk   0.2

9/18/13   GG: rec and rev docket from Probate Court   0.2
TC w/Client; rev email from Client   0.1

9/22/13   GG: TCs w/Client   0.4

9/23/13   GG: TC w/Client   0.1
Draft email to Client   0.3

9/30/13   GG: TC w/Client   0.1

10/4/13   GG: Rec and rev Memorandum & Order on
Father's Motion for Stay; TCs w/Client;
Draft email to Client   0.4
TC w/Cambridge Transcriptions   0.2
TC to Mass Appeals Court   0.1
LF: Confer w/GG re Memorandum & Order   0.3   NC

4

```
Balance due on last bill      $40,446
Payment 8/17/13               $40,446

Current Bill:

Total Hours Expended          96.7
Hours Not charged      -      35.7
Billed Hours                  61.0

61.0 hours @ $350/hour =      $21,350

Plus Expenses:         +      $   182

Total Billed:                 $21,532

Payment 9/11/13        -         7,000


Balance Due                   $14,532
```

5

Law Offices
FONT & GLAZER
20 Melrose Street
Boston, Massachusetts 02116

Telephone (617) 451-2300
Fax (617) 451-6196

Louis P. Font
Gale L. Glazer

FEE AGREEMENT

This Agreement, dated July 18, 2013 is made by and between Javad Ghoreishi, of 77 Pond Ave., Brookline, MA 02445, hereafter referred to as "Client" and Gale L. Glazer, of FONT & GLAZER, hereafter referred to as "Attorney".

1.   The Client retains Attorney Glazer to represent the Client in matters pertaining to post-trial litigation concerning his Norfolk County Probate & Family Court divorce case. These matters may include as attorney deems appropriate in her professional judgment, motions before the trial court and litigation before the Court of Appeals. This Fee Agreement specifically does not include legal services pertaining to litigation before the Supreme Judicial Court, which would require a new Fee Agreement.

2.   The Client shall pay the Attorney legal fees at the rate of $350.00 (Three Hundred and Fifty Dollars) per hour.

3.   The Client agrees that Attorney Glazer may obtain assistance from her law partner Attorney Louis Font in handling this matter, and insofar as Attorney Font provides separate and not duplicative services, the Client agrees to pay Attorney Font's legal fees at the rate of $350.00 (Three Hundred and Fifty Dollars) per hour.

1

4.   The retainer fee for legal services in this case is $25,000.00 (Twenty-Five Thousand Dollars). The Client has this date paid Attorney the sum of $10,000.00 (Ten Thousand Dollars) as partial payment of this $25,000.00 (Twenty-Five Thousand Dollar) retainer fee.

5.   The Client shall pay the Attorney the additional sum of $10,000.00 (Ten Thousand Dollars) toward the retainer fee one week from today, on July 25, 2013; and the Client shall pay the Attorney the additional sum of $5,000.00 (Five Thousand Dollars), to complete payment of the retainer fee, two weeks from today, on August 1, 2013.

6.   The Client understands that the $25,000.00 retainer is not an estimate of the fees that Client may ultimately have to pay to the Attorney.

7.   The retainer of $25,000.00 shall be applied toward 71.4 hours of Attorney time. If more time is required, such additional time shall be billed at the rate of $350/hour. Additional retainer(s) may be required by the Attorney at the Attorney's discretion. At the end of legal representation provided by Attorney, any deficiency not covered by the retainer(s) will be billed. If the amount incurred in legal services is less than the amount of the retainer(s) paid, the Client shall be refunded any excess.

8.   Any time spent relative to the Client's matter including but not limited to telephone calls, drafting pleadings or documents, research, email communications to and from the Client as well as others, review of file materials and documents sent or received, conferences, meetings, preparation for meetings or conferences or court appearances, court appearances, and travel time to and from meetings, conferences and court appearances will be billed on an hourly basis. Time will be billed in multiples of 10ths of an hour. A minimum of 1/10 of an hour shall be billed for each action performed.

2

9.   The Client is responsible to pay all reasonable expenses incurred in handling the aforementioned matter(s), including but not limited to costs of postage, delivery service fees, travel expenses (if any), FAX costs (@ $1/page for faxes sent) and photocopy expenses (@ 10cents/page), as well as expenses of obtaining the trial record, transcribing same, compiling the record and providing same and all briefs or other pleadings to opposing counsel and the Court. The Client is also responsible for paying for any expert fees and expenses, if any. If the Attorney pays any expenses out-of-pocket, the Client shall reimburse the Attorney for same.

10.   Amounts billed or requested, whether fee, retainer, or reimbursement of expenses, are due upon presentation. It is agreed that if any amount billed or requested is not paid within 15 days of the date of mailing, emailing or FAXing of said bill or request to the Client, the Attorney, at the Attorney's discretion, may withdraw from representation and may cease providing services under this Agreement.

11.   Interest will be charged at a rate of 1.00% (one percent) per month for any bill more than thirty (30) days in arrears.

12.   It is impossible to determine in advance the amount of time that will be needed to complete the representation of the Client in this matter, and it is understood that the eventual fee may be more than the initial retainer of $25,000.00.

13.   The Client understands that the Attorney has made no guarantee concerning the outcome of this matter.

14.   No representation is made that any contribution by the adverse party will be obtained toward the Client's legal fees or costs.

15.   Either party may withdraw from this Agreement at any time, by reasonable written notice, prior to resolution of this matter. If the attorney-client relationship is terminated

3

before the conclusion of this matter for any reason, the Attorney may seek full payment at Attorney's hourly rate for the work performed, and the Attorney may seek full payment of expenses incurred by Attorney.

16.   This Agreement shall be enforced in accordance with the laws of the Commonwealth of Massachusetts and shall be enforced by the courts in Massachusetts.

17.   The Client agrees to keep the Attorney timely informed of any changes to the Client's address, phone number(s) and/or other contact information.

18.   This Agreement contains the entire understanding between the Attorney and Client.

19.   A fax, photocopy or scanned copy of this signed document is as valid as the original.

I have read the above Agreement before signing it, understand its terms, and freely intend to be bound by it. I have received a copy of this Agreement at the time of signing.

_____
Client

Dated: July 19, 2013
Brookline, MA.

Agreed to and accepted:

_____
Attorney Gale L. Glazer

Dated: July 19, 2013
Boston, MA.

4

COMMONWEALTH OF MASSACHUSETTS

NORFOLK, ss.   PROBATE & FAMILY COURT
                                                No. 11D0426DR

KAYOKO OBARA,

    Plaintiff,

v.

JAVAD GHOREISHI,

    Defendant.

NOTICE OF APPEAL

The defendant/husband Javad Ghoreishi hereby submits a Notice of Appeal from the Judgment of Contempt filed on October 11, 2013 and Order on Request for Attorney's Fees dated January 29, 2014 and related pre-judgment orders entered by Hon. George F. Phelan.

Respectfully submitted,
JAVAD GHOREISHI
By His Attorney

Michael J. Traft
B.B.O. #500480
Attorney at Law
1 State Street, Suite 1500
Boston, MA 02109
(617) 933-3877

Dated: February 12, 2014

180

MICHAEL J. TRAFT
Attorney at Law
One State Street
Suite 1500
Boston, MA 02109
TEL. (617) 933-3877
FAX (617) 933-3878
mtraft@traftlaw.com

February 12, 2014

Pasquale DeSantis, Esq.
Prince, Lobel & Tye LLP
100 Cambridge Street, Suite 2200
Boston, MA 02114

    RE: Kayoko Obara v. Javad Ghoreishi
         Norfolk Probate & Family Court No. 11D0426DR

Dear Pasquale:

    We have today filed a Notice of Appeal from the Judgment of Contempt. Since our only quarrel is with the award and amount of legal fees I only want to include the transcript of the January 23rd hearing. I also intend to consolidate the two appeals for the purposes of efficiency. If you are in agreement, I can submit the appropriate paperwork and get the appeal in process. I usually use Cambridge Transcriptions to prepare the transcript. Please let me know your thoughts on these issues.

                                     Very Truly Yours,

                                     Michael J. Traft

cc: Javad Ghoreishi

Enclosures

181

MICHAEL J. TRAFT
Attorney at Law
One State Street
Suite 1500
Boston, MA 02109
TEL. (617) 933-3877
FAX (617) 933-3878
mtraft@traftlaw.com

February 12, 2014

VIA HAND DELIVERY

Register of Probate
Norfolk Probate & Family Court
35 Shawmut Road
Canton, MA 02021

      RE: Kayoko Obara v. Javad Ghoreishi
          Norfolk Probate & Family Court No. 11D0426DR

Dear Sir or Madam:

Enclosed please find for filing in the above-captioned matter the Notice of Appeal filed by the defendant/husband Javad Ghoreishi of the Judgment of Contempt filed on October 11, 2013 and Order on Request for Attorney's Fees dated January 29, 2014 and related pre-judgment orders. Please contact me if you have any questions.

                         Very Truly Yours,

                         Michael J. Traft

cc: Pasquale DeSantis, Esq.
     Javad Ghoreishi

COMMONWEALTH OF MASSACHUSETTS
TRIAL COURT

NORFOLK, SS   **PROBATE AND FAMILY COURT**
                                                               DOCKET NO: 11D0426DR

KAYOKO OBARA,	)
Plaintiff	)
	)
v.	)
	)
JAVAD GHOREISHI,	)
Defendant	)
	)

INTERIM DISCOVERY MASTER REPORT AND ORDER

I.   *Appointment*: This Court appointed me Special Master for Discovery pursuant to the
      Order dated March 18, 2019. It is my duty to confer and communicate with counsel
      and the Husband, pro se, to establish a discovery schedule, to address discovery
      disputes and to help the parties resolve such disputes. In the absence of an
      agreement, I have the authority to issue Orders regarding discovery.

II.   *Brief Procedural History*: On March 7, 2016, the Appeals Court vacated, and
      remanded portions of the divorce judgment dated December 12, 2013. Specifically,
      so much of the judgment that orders division of property was vacated and remanded
      for further proceedings and findings, and if appropriate, redistribution of the dental
      practice, including a re-allocation of other assets to the extent necessary to effectuate
      an equitable division of the assets. Additionally, so much of the judgment that orders
      the Husband to pay retroactive child support from May, 2011 to the date of trial was
      vacated and the orders requiring the Husband to pay the Wife's attorney's fees were
      vacated and remanded for further proceedings and findings.

      On February 26, 2019, the matter was scheduled for two days of trial. In an order of
      the same date, this Court noted that the case was not ready for trial as the parties and
      Wife's counsel had failed to comply with the trial scheduling order. The Court further
      noted that the Wife's counsel represented that the Wife is willing to waive any claim
      for child support from May, 2011 to the judgment date, as well as the attorney's fees
      awarded under the judgment. Therefore, the primary issue is the division of property,
      particularly the dental practice. Depending on the value of the dental practice, a
      different division of the assets may be required to effectuate an equitable division.

      In its February 26, 2019 Order, this Court ordered, in relevant part, that the Wife
      produce copies of her 2015-2017 business tax returns with all schedules; the Husband
      forthwith produce documents responsive to the Wife's First Request for Production of
      Documents dated 10/9/18 and the Wife allow access to the dental office to Ed Fererro

Interim Report of the Special Master for Discovery
Obara v. Ghoreishi - Norfolk Probate & Family Court Docket no. 11D0426DR
May 7, 2019
Page 2

of DDS Match Company, or such other expert hired by the Husband, within ten (10) days so the practice may be appraised. Any valuation prepared in connection with this appraisal shall be provided by the Husband to the Wife's counsel within five (5) days of receipt.

III. *Status of Discovery*: In summary, I have performed the following work: (i) reviewed the Wife's request for production of documents pursuant to Rule 34; (ii) had telephone discussions with Attorney Jenney, Wife's counsel; (iii) had telephone discussions with the Husband; (iv) exchanged written correspondence with Attorney Jenney; (v) exchanged written correspondence with the Husband; and, (vi) reviewed the Court file for additional relevant orders concerning discovery. After a review of all of these records and corresponding with the Husband and Attorney Jenney, I requested and received responsive documents from each side.

Upon receipt of documents from the Husband, I reviewed the documents for responsiveness and completeness to the Wife's Rule 34 Request for Production of Documents. The responsive documents were organized to be consistent with the numbered requests of Attorney Jenney's Rule 34 request and forwarded to Attorney Jenney with a copy to the Husband.

I received a letter from Attorney Jenney on May 6, 2019, which letter copied the Husband and also forwarded by me to the Husband[1] in which Attorney Jenney references the transfer of Unit 77-406 at the Brook House complex by the Husband to a third-party purchaser, Ms. Nancy Reimer. According to the deed recorded with the Registry of Deeds, the consideration for the sale of Unit 77-406 was $719,000. Attorney Jenney alleges that the Husband did not own Unit 77-406 at the time of transfer to the third-party purchaser. Attorney Jenney argues that Unit 77-406 remained "marital property" subject to division since the Appeals Court remanded the case.

In a telephone conference on May 6, 2019, Attorney Jenney advised me that there are additional documents which he seeks from the Husband but as of the writing of this report, I have not received additional correspondence

Attorney Jenney represented that he had previously provided the Husband with the Wife's income tax returns, however, the Husband said he never received them. At my request, on May 6, 2019, Attorney Jenney produced the Wife's income tax returns for 2017 and 2018. Attorney Jenney has represented to me that he will provide the Wife's 2015 and 2016 income tax returns as well.

---

[1] Attorney Jenney noted in the cc line of the letter an email address for the Husband as follows: javadghoreishi@comcast.net. At the Husband's request, I have been corresponding with him using the following email address: javad.ghoreishi@rcn.com. I forwarded Attorney Jenney's May 6, 2019 letter as well as Ms. Obara's 2017 and 2018 income tax returns to Tthe Husband at his RCN email address to ensure he received copies.

Interim Report of the Special Master for Discovery
Obara v. Ghoreishi - Norfolk Probate & Family Court Docket no. 11D0426DR
May 7, 2019
Page 3

The Husband reports having issued three different subpoenas *duces tecum* during this litigation – two subpoenas dated July 20, 2018 and one subpoena dated December 4, 2017 – none of the copies provided to me were signed.

In his first July 20, 2018 subpoena the Husband seeks the establishment of an escrow account to hold all of the money paid by the Husband pursuant to the Judgment of Divorce and on remand. Since this is not a proper request pursuant to a subpoena duces tecum I do not make any orders concerning this request.

In his second subpoena dated July 20, 2018 the Husband seeks (i) the ability to inspect several Persian rugs which he claims are in the possession of the Wife as well as the Wife's dental practice; (ii) a list of patient schedules and number of days of actual patient treatment; (iii) number of days engaging with other dental office activities (lab work, patient record writing, etc.); a complete list of the items removed when she moved out of 77 Pond Avenue in September, 2011; and, a complete list of existing dental units, dental lab and lab equipment; instruments; dental materials, dental office furniture; computers and copy machines.

In the subpoena dated December 4, 2017, the Husband seeks "Original deed or a 300 ppm copy picture xerox copy" of the original deed for 77 Pond Avenue, No. 201, Dedham MA and 77 Pond Avenue NR (also known as units 102 and 103), Brookline, MA.

IV. *Recommendations/Orders*:

1. I reserve all recommendations and orders regarding the parties' ongoing discovery dispute in this current litigation, as well as which party, if either, acted in bad faith in connection with discovery leading up to the ultimate disposition of this matter.

2. I likewise reserve all recommendations and orders regarding final assessment of special master fees for each party. Until such further order from myself, or this Court, the Parties shall continue to pay for my services equally. Each party has paid an initial retainer of $3,000 for a total of $6,000 towards my fees.

3. Both parties shall continue to cooperate with me in seeking to resolve discovery disputes.

4. At the present time, I have not received confirmation from the Husband as to whether or not he still seeks access to the dental practice for valuation purposes. I have written to the Husband on two occasions[2] requesting his position on the matter and although, he has responded to my emails, the Husband has not responded to this

---

[2] I emailed the Husband on May 1, 2019 and on May 2, 2019 regarding this specific issue.

Interim Report of the Special Master for Discovery
Obara v. Ghoreishi - Norfolk Probate & Family Court Docket no. 11D0426DR
May 7, 2019
Page 4

specific question. Certain of the Husband's requests included in his July 20, 2018 subpoena duces tecum would relate to the work of a business valuator. Accordingly, confirmation of whether or not the Husband has retained an expert and seeks access to the dental practice is relevant.

> a. The Husband shall notify Attorney Jenney and me via email on or before **Monday, May 14, 2019**, the name and address of any expert retained by the Husband to value the dental practice and whether or not he seeks access to the dental practice. If the Husband seeks access to the practice, he shall identify in his email 3 dates with proposed 2-hour blocks of time as to when he is available to visit the practice – all 3 proposed dates shall be after **May 24, 2019**. When choosing dates and times, the Husband shall be mindful of minimizing the potential disruption to the Wife's practice. Reasonable efforts shall be made by the Wife to accommodate the proposed dates and times by the Husband. Attorney Jenney shall respond to the Husband's email within **72 hours** of the date stamp on the Husband's email. Attorney Jenney shall either (i) confirm a date and time as proposed by the Husband or (ii) propose 3 alternate dates with proposed 2-hour blocks of time. The Husband shall then pick one of the 3 days and times proposed by the Wife and shall confirm via email to Attorney Jenney and myself the specific dates/times within 72 hours of the date stamp on Attorney Jenney's email.

> b. If the Husband will be visiting the dental practice with his business valuator expert, he shall notify Attorney Jenney via email with a copy to me **at least 48 hours** prior to the scheduled walkthrough and provide the name of the individual who will be in attendance with the Husband. The Husband and any expert may be required to sign a confidentiality agreement prior to reviewing any business records of the practice.

> c. Either party may make arrangements and pay for a police officer to be present during the Husband's walk through. Notification that such arrangements have been made shall be provided to the other party (or, Attorney Jenney) **at least 24 hours** prior to the walkthrough of the dental practice.

5. On or before **May 24, 2019**, the Husband shall produce the first 3 pages of his business state income tax return for year 2018 (The 2018 business tax return previously produced starts on Schedule A, page 2).

6. On or before **May 24, 2019**, the Wife, through her counsel, shall provide a written response to items numbered 1-7 and 11 to the Husband's subpoena dated July 20, 2018. For items 1-7, the Wife's response shall indicate if she is in possession of said item and if so, where the item is located.

Interim Report of the Special Master for Discovery
Obara v. Ghoreishi - Norfolk Probate & Family Court Docket no. 11D0426DR
May 7, 2019
Page 5

7. As noted above under *Brief Procedural History*, I decline to enter Orders concerning the Husband's subpoena dated July 20, 2018 as it seeks the implementation of an escrow account which is outside the authority of this special master.

8. With regards to the Husband's subpoena dated December 4, 2017 seeking the "original" deed or "300 ppm color copy" of the deed for certain properties, the best evidence of these records is on file at the Norfolk Registry of Deeds and may be obtained directly by the Husband – whether on line or in person.

9. With the exception of depositions requiring live testimony, all discovery (including but not limited to, Rule 34 requests for documents; request for interrogatories; requests for admissions; records only subpoenas; and, requests to inspect) shall be completed by **June 28, 2019**. All requests shall be served in a timely manner to ensure that the dates for compliance occur prior to the discovery deadline.

10. All depositions requiring live testimony shall be completed by **August 1, 2019**.

Respectfully submitted,

Jennifer C. Roman, Esquire
Hoffman Law Group
501 Providence Highway
Norwood, MA 02062
Phone: (781) 440-9500
Dated: May 7, 2019   Email: jroman@jhoffmanlaw.com

Interim Report of the Special Master for Discovery
Obara v. Ghoreishi - Norfolk Probate & Family Court Docket no. 11D0426DR
May 7, 2019
Page 6

CERTIFICATE OF SERVICE

I, Jennifer C. Roman, do hereby certify that on this 7th day of May, 2019, I served the foregoing Interim Discovery Master Report and Order on the attorney for the Plaintiff via email and first class mail as follows:

John B. Jenney, Esquire
10 Glen Road
Wayland, MA 01778
jbiffjenney@aol.com

and on the Defendant, Javad Ghoreishi, (pro se) via email and first-class mail to him at:

Dr. Javad Ghoreishi
77 Pond Avenue, Apt. 201
Brookline, MA 02445
javad.ghoreishi@rcn.com

Jennifer C. Roman

Patent No.

WO 2014/199243 A1

Javad Ghoreishi

INVENTOR

WORLD PATENT

The Commissioner of Patents has received an application for a new and useful invention. The requirements of the Patent Act having been complied with, it has been determined that a patent on the invention, known as

TOPICAL THERAPEUTIC COMPOSITION AND PALLIATIVE TREATMENT METHOD

shall be granted under the laws of the WIPO. Therefore, this Patent grants to the applicant or legal representatives of said applicant the exclusive right, privilege, and liberty of making, constructing, using and vending to others in the WIPO.

M C Henry

Attesting Officer

December 18, 2014
Date of Issue

LAW OFFICE

HELMAN & NEUSTADT
1340 CENTRE STREET, SUITE 205
NEWTON CENTRE, MASSACHUSETTS 02459

JONATHAN S. HELMAN
PAUL S. NEUSTADT

617 243-0000
FACSIMILE: 617-243-0429

July 16, 2013

Dr. Javad Ghoreishi
77 Pond Avenue, Unit No. 201
Brookline, Massachusetts 02445

Re: Judgment/Appeal/Motion to Stay Judgment

Dear Javad,

It is important that I reiterate, and place in writing, some of the salient points of our discussion this afternoon. I will be as direct and succinct as possible.

1. While I clearly recognize that this is your case and your life, I too feel a profound disappointment in Judge Phalen's Judgment and Findings of Fact.

2. I understand that you wish to claim an appeal of the Judgment to the Massachusetts Appeals Court.

3. I do not handle appeals, and I urge you to engage an appellate lawyer *immediately*!

4. The Notice of Appeals *must* be filed at the Norfolk Probate and Family Court *no later than 30 days after the date the Judgment is docketed.* It is not the date of the Judgment, but the docketing that is the measuring time. Again, consult with an appellate lawyer. You cannot file the Notice of Appeal until the Judgment is docketed which is a technical procedural step. I do not know if your Judgment is docketed yet. You can find out by calling, or going to, the Court.

5. There are many steps after you file the Notice of Appeal; you should engage counsel.

6. If you wish to file a Motion to Stay Execution of the Judgment Pending Appeal, you must file the Motion and have it heard by Judge Phalen before August 1st which is the date you are required to vacate the office according to the Judgment. Again this should be done by your new lawyer.

Sincerely,

JONATHAN S. HELMAN

10/31/18   06-21√

COMMONWEALTH OF MASSACHUSETTS

NORFOLK, SS.   SUPERIOR COURT 19-0824-8/8/18)
                                               CIVIL ACTION NO. ~~17 0676~~

)   Motion
JAVAD GHOREISHI   )   Allowed ,
)   (Hearing occured
      Plaintiff.   )   6/18/2019)
)
      v.   )
)
JOHN B. JENNEY   )
      Defendant   )

REQUEST FOR HEARING

The Plaintiff, Javad Ghoreishi, requests for a status review and hearing on the Plaintiff's complaint against John B Jenney.

NOTIFIED 06-21-19
(NS)
-J.G.
-J.B.J.

Respectfully submitted

Javad Ghoreishi
77 Pond Avenue # 201
Brookline, MA 02445
Phone: 617-651-1500
javadghoreishi@comcast.net,

Date: October 30 , 201

certificate of Service

I, Javad Ghoreishi, Pro Se, hereby certify that on October 30, 2018, I served forgoing document on defendant, John B Jenney Esq., by first class mail.

_____
Javad Ghoreishi

John B Jenney
10 Glen Road
Wayland, MA 01778

191

COMMONWEALTH OF MASSACHUSETTS

SUFFOLK, ss

SUPERIOR COURT
CA NO. 19-0874-B

JAVAD GHOREISHI

Notified 06-21-19 (N²
- J.G.
- J.B.J.

v.

JOHN B. JENNEY

MEMORANDUM OF DECISION AND
ORDER ON MOTION FOR SUMMARY JUDGMENT

Background Undisputed Facts of Record

This case was originally filed in Norfolk County,[1] and stems from a divorce action

pending in the Norfolk Probate and Family Court (Divorce Action).

Each party here is representing himself. Plaintiff Ghoreishi is a dentist, and the defendant

in the Divorce Action. Defendant Jenney is the attorney for Ghoreishi's wife Kayoko Obara,

also a dentist and the plaintiff in the Divorce Action. A portion of the July, 2013 Judgment of

Divorce Nisi (Nisi), regarding division of property and a related set of orders, was vacated and

remanded by the Appeals Court in March, 2016. Obara v. Ghoreishi, 89 Mass. 1110 (2016)(Rule

1:28 decision).

The disputed property at issue is a dental practice consisting of an office condominium

and equipment, which Ghoreishi and Obara shared prior to the Divorce Action. The 2013 Nisi

had awarded that practice to Obara. The Appeals Court ruled that the judgment below failed

---

[1]   Norfolk Civil Action No. 17-0676, transferred here by order of March 5, 2019, pursuant to a
motion by the Plaintiff in January, 2019, as an accommodation to his medical condition and use of a motorized
scooter for transportation. Docket Papers 15-16. Elsewhere Ghoreishi states that he is "wheelchair bound due to MS
since June of 2000." Complaint, para. 15. The summary judgment pleadings were filed in June-September, 2018.
There is otherwise no explanation on the record before me for the delay in hearing the Motion for Summary
Judgment.

1

meaningfully to consider the impact of Ghoreishi's relocation from that practice on his employability and opportunity for future acquisition of capital assets and income. Defendant Jenney reported at the hearing before me that the Divorce Action does not yet have a firm retrial date; a final trial conference is currently set for August 1, 2019. Ghoreishi has apparently not been allowed to practice dentistry in the disputed office space since October, 2013, but still seeks to regain that access. See, for example, Amended Complaint, at Exhibit #10.

The parties have also been involved in another proceeding arising out of the remanded Divorce Action, which is the subject of the Amended Complaint in this case. In November, 2016, Attorney Jenney wrote a letter to the Board of Registration in Dentisty (the Board). In that letter Jenney acknowledged he represented Obara in "some civil litigation concerning a dental office," that both sides "claim an interest in [the] dental office," and that "both claims are valid." Jenney then questioned Ghoreishi's "physical ability to practice dentistry," stating that Ghoreishi's "knowledge and skill are not in question – he has been a competent dentist for decades."

Jenney went on to report to the Board that, as is undisputed: Ghoreishi has been diagnosed with multiple sclerosis (MS); has "lost his lower body strength;" and receives certain disability insurance payments as a result. Jenney stated that "the [Probate] court has suggested we divide the office into two [separate] offices," but "[b]efore we proceed with construction cost, I am asking a determination from the Board of registration as to the limits, if any, and any impediments his physical health may play in his ability to resume practice," adding "he has been out of practice for over three years."

As represented by Jenney at the hearing before me, and also in filings with the Probate Court, the Board authored a proposed "Consent Agreement for Stayed Probation" (Proposed

2

Consent Agreement) establishing a procedure for evaluating Ghoreishi's capacity to continue

practicing dentistry. Motion, Paper 10, at Exhibit D. However, Ghoreishi did not agree to

participate in the proposed procedure. The summary judgment record contains no reliable

information as to the current status of Ghoreishi's license, despite a provision in the Proposed

Consent Agreement that "failure to fulfill the requirements of [the procedure] may result in the

imposition of discipline by the Board." Id., at para. 3.

Claims and Defenses

Ghoreishi's Amended Complaint (Complaint) in four counts focuses primarily on

Jenney's letter to the Board. He claims: Defamation/Libel; Intimidation/humiliation; Violation

of Code of Ethics, and Violation of American with Disability Act (ADA). Paper 3. Ghoreishi's

central theory is that Jenny's letter to the Board is false, and that Jenney wrote the letter (and

took several other actions described below) for the wrongful purpose of bringing Board

disciplinary action against Ghoreishi, and getting his license to practice dentistry revoked,

thereby preventing Ghoreishi from "regaining the use of the modified dental office,"[2] to the

advantage of Jenney's client Obara in the Divorce Action. Complaint, paras. 1, 22-23, 27, 37.

Jenney's defense to the claims is that the letter to the Board was written "within the

parameters of [the Divorce Action]," for which he is protected by absolute immunity from suit.

Memorandum of Law (within Paper 10), at page 1. In response, Ghoreishi claims that the issue

before the court is "one of intentional and purposeful act to block and deter Appeals Court's

decision and order," (Response (Paper 12), at page 1), and that "Defendant's action is an issue of

civil matter for his private gain." Memorandum in Opposition (Paper 14) at page 2.

---

[2]   It appears undisputed in this record that the condominium dental practice asset in question was "modified" before the Divorce Action to provide accommodation to Ghoreishi's physical limitations from MS. However, the summary judgment record does not describe the modifications.

3

The question, then, is whether Jenney is able to demonstrate at this stage of the case that no material disputes of fact exist as to Ghoreeshi's claims, and that Jenney is entitled to judgment as a matter of law, pursuant to Mass.R.Civ.P. 56(b). Following hearing June 18, 2019, and thorough review of all materials submitted by the parties,[3] Jenney's Motion for Summary Judgment (Paper 10) is **ALLOWED.**

Discussion

There is no question that the Divorce Action has been bitterly fought. However, Jenney's advocacy on behalf of his client, including commentary within pleadings or hearings in Probate Court, however intemperate that commentary may appear to Ghoreishi, is absolutely privileged as a matter of civil tort law. Doe v. Nutter, McClennen & Fish, 41 Mass. App. Ct. 137, 140-141 (1996) and cases cited. Examples of Jenney's actions or statements in this category include the allegation that he called Ghoreishi "fraudulent or a liar" in a pleading filed in the Divorce Action (Complaint, para. 2 and Exhibit #2); that Jenney sought findings and temporary orders from the Probate Court with respect to the Board proceeding, Complaint Exhibit #5; and that Jenney made unflattering statements about Ghoreishi in email discussions between counsel in the Divorce Action, as well as in open court. Complaint, paras. 24, 32-35, and Exhibit #7. Ghoreishi's only potential remedy for these advocacy remarks by Jenney (which Ghoreishi sometimes labels as "contemptuous,") (Complaint at para. 10), would lie within the discretion of the Probate Court in which the statements were made.

---

[3] The Complaint references and attaches seven exhibits, Exhibit #1 of which is Jenney's letter to the Board. The Motion and Memorandum (Paper 10) attaches five exhibits. The Response (opposition) and Memorandum (Papers 12-14) add certain other materials. There is significant redundancy within these papers. Mindful that these parties (one a dentist and one a Probate and Family Court practitioner) are representing themselves in Superior Court, all of these materials have been considered.

4

That said, the Complaint squarely raises the question of whether litigation counsel's referral of an issue to a regulatory body outside the court in which the trial matter is pending is also clothed in immunity, as "in the conduct of litigation," when the statements "relate to that proceeding." Sriberg v. Raymond, 370 Mass. 105, 108-109 (1976). I rule that in the circumstances presented here, it is. Statements made to police officers or prosecutors, by attorneys or witnesses, have long been considered absolutely privileged from liability "if pertinent to the matter in hearing." Correllas v. Viveiros, 410 Mass. 314, 320-322 (1991); Sriberg, 370 Mass. at 109 ("The public policy of permitting attorneys complete freedom of expression and candor in communications in their efforts to secure justice for their clients commends itself to us"). "[W]ords spoken by a witness in the course of judicial proceedings which are pertinent to the matter in hearing are absolutely privileged, even if uttered maliciously or in bad faith. . . . and the words 'pertinent to the proceedings' are not to be construed narrowly." Robert L. Sullivan, D.D.S., P.C. v. Birmingham, 11 Mass. App. Ct. 359, 362 (1981)(citations omitted).

Of course, our law recognizes that the litigation privilege may be abused by unnecessary or excessive publication. Id., at 365-366. However, that is not the situation presented by this record. Correllas, 410 Mass. at 322-324 ("A careful, fact-specific analysis will better balance the right of a plaintiff to preserve his or her reputation from defamatory accusations, with the right of society to secure the testimony of a witness in proposed and in actual judicial proceedings without the parity or witness laboring under th threat of a civil suit.") Ghoreishi's physical ability to practice dentistry was clearly "pertinent to the matter in hearing" in the Probate Court (fair apportionment of the asset of the dental practice), and the Board was the appropriate place to seek clarification of that issue. Since the tort of defamation is the publication of material by

5

one without a privilege to do so, this body of law defeats Count I of the Complaint. Correllas, 410 Mass. at 319.

So too Count II, for "Intimidation/humiliation," which I read to be attempting to state a claim for intentional infliction of emotional distress. This tort requires as a critical element that the accused actor is not otherwise privileged to engage in the challenged conduct. Agis v. Howard Johnson, 371 Mass. 140, 144-145 (1976). Existence of a legal tort duty is a question of law, which may be resolved by summary judgment. Afarian v. Massachusetts Elec. Co., 449 Mass. 257, 261 (2007), citing Jupin v. Kask, 447 Mass. 141, 146 (2006). And, because "[a] privilege which protected an individual from liability for defamation would be of little value if the individual were subject to liability under a different theory of tort," Correllas, 410 Mass. at 324, summary judgment is proper on this claim as well. Robert L. Sullivan, 11 Mass. App. Ct. at 367.

At paragraphs 36-37 of the Complaint Ghoreishi correctly identifies a Rule of Professional Conduct for lawyers in the Commonwealth which states that a lawyer shall not "present, participate in presenting, or threaten to present criminal or disciplinary charges solely to obtain an advantage in a private civil matter." SJC Rule 3:07, DR 3.4(h)(1998). The Consent Agreement proposed by the Board clearly speaks in terms of a "Complaint pending against [Ghoreishi's] License before the Board [with docket number]," "Probation," and "Stayed Probation." Motion Exhibit D, at paras. 1, 4. Ghoreishi describes the Board proceedings as "[d]efendant's action to assassinate plaintiff's professional life." Memorandum in Opposition, at page 3.

I agree proceedings before the Board could fairly be characterized as disciplinary. However, ethical rules do not provide an independent cause of action in a civil dispute. Fishman

6

v. Brooks, 396 Mass. 643, 649-650 (1986); Robert L. Sullivan, 11 Mass. App. Ct. at 368-369. For this reason, Count III of the Complaint cannot survive summary judgment.

Nor do these undisputed facts rise to a claim against Jenney under federal (or state) statutory disability discrimination law. Complaint at paras. 39-40. Jenney's privileged acts and statements presented by this record merely consisted of offering questions or arguments about Ghoreishi's "physical ability to practice dentistry," a fact potentially relevant to fair property distribution in the Divorce Action. Jenney was not a decision-maker about either Ghoreishi's health or his employment, and as such had no legal duty to Ghoreishi under these statutes. Summary judgment is appropriate on Count IV.

Plaintiff erroneously suggests that "[m]ore discovery or possible witness testimony at trial might be necessary to actually establish defendant's action for his private gain. . . . The necessary facts should be presented at trial before a trier of fact to determine its validity." Memorandum in Opposition, at page 5. That is not the standard to be applied to the Motion. Rule 56 of our Rules of Civil Procedure precludes trial when the undisputed record to date demonstrates a party is entitled to judgment as a matter of law. Additional (undescribed) discovery or possible (unidentified) witness testimony cannot defeat such a Motion at this stage of the case.

Conclusion

For all of these reasons, summary judgment is **ALLOWED** on each of the four Counts of the Amended Complaint, and the case is **dismissed with prejudice**.

SO ORDERED.

Dated: June 21, 2019

Christine M. Roach

7

tinuing controversy over the suspension of embattled Suffolk Register
D. Arroyo.

Governor Charlie Baker's office issued a statement shortly before Medonis, a top
administrator in the troubled Probate and Family Court since 2013, was
scheduled to face questions in a confirmation hearing before the Governor's
Council.

"Since learning of controversial personnel matters, Governor Baker and
Lieutenant Governor Polito have granted Linda Medonis' request to withdraw
her nomination," Lizzy Guyton, Baker's communications director, said in a
statement. "The administration thanks attorney Medonis for her willingness to
serve as a justice on the court."

Stay updated, right in your news feed.

Most Popular In Metro

 Report names 12 at Choate Rosemary Hall who allegedly abused students

In almost all of the cases, school officials failed to report sexual misconduct to
the authorities when the accusations first surfaced and quietly fired teachers or allowed
them to resign. MORE...

 Private schools, painful secrets

More than 200 victims. At least 90 legal claims. At least 67 private schools in
New England. This is the story of hundreds of students sexually abused by
staffers, and emerging from decades of silence today. MORE...

Judicial nominee withdraws hours before confirmation hearing

SUZANNE KREITER/GLOBE STAFF

Felix Arroyo, seen at a press conference this month, was suspended from his job as Suffolk register.

By **Andrew Ryan** | GLOBE STAFF APRIL 12, 2017

Judicial nominee Linda M. Medonis abruptly withdrew her nomination hours

Continue Reading ⌄

COMMONWEALTH OF MASSACHUSETTS
THE TRIAL COURT
PROBATE AND FAMILY COURT DEPARTMENT

Norfolk Division   **Docket No.   11D0426**

Kayoko Obara, Plaintiff

v.

Javad Ghoreishi, Defendant

ORDER
(On Complaint for Contempt filed 3/7/19)

This matter came before the Court today for hearing. Plaintiff appeared and was represented by Attorney John B. Jenney. Defendant appeared and represented himself. Plaintiff alleges Defendant has not complied with outstanding discovery. There have been on-going discovery disputes between the parties. This matter was scheduled for a remand trial on February 26, 2019 and February 27, 2019, but cancelled as the parties failed to comply with the trial scheduling order and it was not ready for trial.

After hearing, it is **ORDERED THAT:**

1. A separate order shall issue appointing a discovery master.

2. The Rule 16 Conference scheduled for March 28, 2019 at 9:00 a.m. is rescheduled to **May 9, 2019 at 9:00 a.m.**

Date: 3/18/19

_____
Paul M. Cronan, Associate Justice
Norfolk Probate & Family Court

Page 1 of 1

201

COMMONWEALTH OF MASSACHUSETTS
THE TRIAL COURT
PROBATE AND FAMILY COURT DEPARTMENT

Norfolk Division   Docket No. 11D0426

Kayoko Obara, Plaintiff

v.

Javad Ghoreishi, Defendant

TEMPORARY ORDER APPOINTING SPECIAL MASTER FOR DISCOVERY

After hearing from the parties and reviewing the conduct of the proceedings, it is hereby ORDERED as follows:

1. Jennifer Roman, Esq. of Hoffman Law Group, 501 Providence Highway, Norwood, MA 02062 (781) 440-9500 is appointed to serve as Special Master for Discovery (hereinafter "Discovery Master").

2. All disputes regarding all party and non-party discovery matters in the above-entitled cases are hereby referred to the Discovery Master for decision. The Discovery Master shall establish a discovery schedule as she sees fit.

3. The Discovery Master shall confer with counsel for the purpose of resolving any discovery disputes or establishing a discovery schedule. The Discovery Master's decisions shall be reduced to writing with copies provided to all counsel of record.

4. The parties shall comply with the terms of any discovery order entered by the Discovery Master, provided that any party may file with the court a written objection to any order entered by the Discovery Master within three (3) business days of the receipt of the order by counsel. In the event an objection is filed, the Discovery Master's order shall be stayed pending a ruling by the court and an expedited hearing shall be held on the objection. The objection shall be served on the Discovery Master but the Discovery Master need not attend any hearing on the objection unless requested to do so by the Court. If the Court finds that a party has acted in bad faith or in an unreasonable manner, the offending party may be assessed the total cost of the proceedings related to the objection to the Discovery Master's order.

5. The Discovery Master shall be compensated for her time and expenses at her usual hourly rate and may require payment of a reasonable retainer. The parties shall initially bear the cost of the Discovery Master equally. The Court expressly reserves the question of final responsibility for the fees and costs of the Discovery Master. The issue of final responsibility shall be determined by the Court after consideration of the written recommendation of the Discovery Master.

6. This Order of Reference to the Discovery Master shall remain in effect through final judgment in the above-entitled action, unless earlier modified by Order of the Court.

7. The Plaintiff is represented by Attorney John B. Jenney, Esq. (508) 358-7829 and the Defendant is pro se.

March 18, 2019
DATE

PAUL M. CRONAN, JUSTICE

COMMONWEALTH OF MASSACHUSETTS
THE TRIAL COURT

SUFFOLK, SS

HOUSING COURT DEPARTMENT
EASTERN DIVISION
Docket No. 18-SP-001

****

Javad Ghoreishi
PLAINTIFF

v.

Devon Hincapie and Juan Hincapie
DEFENDANTS
****

FINDINGS OF FACT, RULINGS OF LAW,
AND ORDER FOR JUDGMENT

This is a summary process action in which Plaintiff Javad Ghoreishi ("Plaintiff") is

seeking to recover possession of the condominium unit he manages at 77 Pond Avenue, Apt.

406, Brookline, Massachusetts (the "premises") from Defendants Devon Hincapie and Juan

Hincapie ("Defendants") and monetary damages based on Defendants' failure to pay rent.

Defendants filed a written Answer and Counterclaims. All parties appeared at a trial on the

merits which was held on April 19, 2018 and were self-represented.

Based upon all the credible testimony and evidence presented at trial, and the reasonable

inferences drawn therefrom, the Court finds as follows: The premises is located within a large

multi-unit complex consisting of hundreds of individually owned condominiums managed by a

condominium trust. There is no dispute that Plaintiff manages the unit for the owner,

Mohammad Kochak ("Owner"), and performs management duties such as collecting rent,

1

About the Author

Dr. Javad Ghoreishi

was born in Iran, Tehran, five years after a coup against democratically elected prime minister Mohammad Mosadegh. My father died when I was five years old, and left six children behind him, we were all raised by a single mother. My mother was a philanthropist, characteristically against injustice, and a community-oriented woman. I learned a lot from my mother about being a humanist and have always tried to be the same way. I was a first class athlete and played on my high school's basketball team,

Tehran University's basketball team, and a famous basketball club in the city in which I lived in at that time. I studied dentistry and earned a dental degree in 1986 at the most prestigious university in Iran, (Tehran University). I was always a rebel against injustice, and I escaped from a brutal regime in Iran to come to the United States. I did research in Preventive Dentistry and Microbiology, I had a successful dental practice in Brookline Massachusetts, and I lost my dental practice in a divorce due to an insidious judgment by a perfidious judge. I contested the insidious judgment at the Appellate Court. I won the contest, and in 2016, the case was remanded for redivision of marital assets including my dental office, for the remand retrial. This time I had a despot as a judge, after four years of the remand case for retrial, finally the retrial was held in January of 2020. The despot has not found a way to crucify me as of yet August 2020.

During the divorce process, in 2013 and 2014 I patented two pharmaceutical Creams at USPTO, and WIPO (World Intellectual Property Organization) and after obtaining the patents, I formed a Pharmaceutical company (Batool Pharma International Inc.).

In 2019, I obtained two provisional patents. The first one was for toothpaste and the second one an Ulnar Cushion to prevent numbness of arms and fingertips while seated for a prolonged time.

Acknowledgments

In memory of my dearest friend Audel Roozdar
who taught me to fight for justice, never give up, and to resist.

My special gratitude to Shimon Segal
for his enumerable physical and mental support during my
struggles.

And my appreciation to my friends
Dr. Mohammad Reza Koochack Entezar
Ray Rezania
my sister Fatemeh Ghoreishi
and to all my other friends who helped me during my struggles.

Special acknowledgment to my PCAs,
Ronald Robinson and Venesha Aljoe.

Lightning Source UK Ltd.
Milton Keynes UK
UKHW020628040121
376386UK00012B/1111